CHERRY PICKING

CHERRY PICKING

LIFE BETWEEN THE STICKS

STEVE CHERRY

WITH JONATHAN NICHOLAS

The Book Guild Ltd

First published in Great Britain in 2018 by
The Book Guild Ltd
9 Priory Business Park
Wistow Road, Kibworth
Leicestershire, LE8 0RX
Freephone: 0800 999 2982
www.bookguild.co.uk
Email: info@bookguild.co.uk
Twitter: @bookguild

Typeset in Adobe Garamond Pro

Printed and bound in Great Britain by CPI Group (UK) Ltd, Croydon, CR0 4YY

ISBN 978 1912575 831

British Library Cataloguing in Publication Data.
A catalogue record for this book is available from the British Library.

To Mum and Dad,
for the sacrifices they made and for giving me such a great life.

Steve Cherry and Jonathan Nicholas

Steve Cherry was born in 1960 into a large family in the Nottinghamshire pit village of Calverton. It was initially assumed he would follow his father and brother into the nearby pit until very early on it was clear he had a special relationship with football. More particularly he wanted to handle the ball rather than simply kick it, and this quickly became his main obsession in life. At the age of fifteen he was already goalkeeping in the local colliery team playing with and against full grown miners when he was spotted by a scout from Derby County, then in the top table of English football. He signed as a schoolboy before turning professional, and was capped for England several times in his youth before eventually winning Derby County's Player of the Year in 1983. He then played for Walsall, again winning Player of the Year, before heading south for Plymouth Argyle where he also distinguished himself by winning Player of the Year. After a short time at Chesterfield he joined the boyhood club of his dreams, Notts County, just after Neil Warnock arrived. County progressed from the bottom of Division Three up to the top of English football via two Wembley play-off wins, and yet again Steve won Player of the Year. He left Notts in 1995 for a return to Plymouth Argyle via Watford, then Rotherham United, Rushden & Diamonds, and several other clubs. In his later years Steve used his love of the game to coach young lads in many different teams until only recently hanging up his boots.

Steve worked with some of the best football managers in the business including Brian Clough and Neil Warnock, obtaining a great insight into how they worked and motivated their teams. He played against some of the greats of English football and distinguished himself at every club he played for in a career that spanned more than thirty years. He played for a dozen clubs in

743 League games and is still fondly remembered and welcomed back at all of them.

'*Cherry Picking – Life between the Sticks*' is a detailed, frank, and often hilarious glimpse into Steve's life, his love of the game, and three very important decades in English football. It is an unmissable read for all fans of the beautiful game, and general readers of biography and autobiography.

Jonathan Nicholas began professional writing in 2011 and has written five books, all of which are non-fiction. He had a column in *Police Review* magazine, has travelled extensively, and spent thirty years as a police officer before becoming a writer.

Acknowledgements

I'd like to send a huge thank you to everyone involved in any way however small in my football career. I've mentioned many of the important people throughout the book but some deserve a special mention. My Mum and Dad of course, because without them none of it would have ever happened; I miss you both. To my sister Lynne Guy, thank you for the great reminders of our happy childhood days, and my good friend Tony Grahame for some of the later information. Thanks to Andy Widdowson and a massive thanks to John and Amanda Males, Jonny Hubbard and the rest of the staff at The Queens Head, Watnall, for allowing us to sit there every week filling up an entire table with all my photos and football memorabilia! I'm hugely indebted to Jonathan Nicholas, my ghost writer, for having the skill and patience to turn all my memories into such a fantastic book, and also to Jeremy Thompson and his wonderful team at The Book Guild for creating it. Extract from *Fever Pitch* by Nick Hornby, published by Penguin, 2000. Copyright Nick Hornby. Reproduced by permission of the author c/o Rogers, Coleridge & White Ltd., 20 Powis Mews, London W11 1JN. Thank you to Mike Sassi at the Nottingham Post for some of the photographs, to Notts County Football Club, Chris Adams and Lawrence Matheson at Reach plc, and John Sumpter at JMS Photography.

Finally, I'd like to say a very special thank you to my darling wife Fiona for her never-ending love and support.

'I fell in love with football as I was later to fall in love with women: suddenly, inexplicably, uncritically, giving no thought to the pain or disruption it would bring with it.'

Nick Hornby, 'Fever Pitch'.

1

I was screaming in agony, and not for the first time. Should I get up, or stay where I was? I'd endured this kind of pain before, and usually someone always came to help me, but not this time. Couldn't they hear me? Why was I being ignored? I was lying there all alone, in total darkness, terrified. This wasn't a dream, it was real. So I screamed again as the pain continued. How could they leave me to suffer like this? Eventually I heard someone coming and I was picked up, but this time it was different. There was shouting and banging as the lights came on, and I was pressed so tightly against my mother's chest I could hardly breathe. She couldn't rouse my brother Robert in the next bed and was shaking him violently. Then there was an awful smell that was making us all cough…I didn't know it, but the house was burning. Smoke and flames were reaching up the stairs and would soon trap us all on the landing. Robert eventually woke up, and then my sister Lynne. My dad led my mum and his family down the stairs and into the safety of the front garden. Thankfully my other older siblings no longer lived at home.

The disastrous house fire at 41 Seely Avenue, Calverton, Nottinghamshire early in 1963 could so easily have caused multiple fatalities, but for the cries of a teething toddler. I don't remember any of it of course, I was only two, but it was lucky I had a good pair of lungs and a low pain threshold at the time! My brother Robert had gone to bed in the same room as me after having some friends around and was supposedly babysitting me and my sister while my mum and dad were at Calverton Miner's Welfare. The fire brigade later said it was most probably caused by a discarded cigarette in the settee which had begun slowly but once taken hold it had spread very quickly. My mum and dad had clearly failed to notice it when they came home, and had gone straight to bed. My mum, who was woken up by my screaming, told me later there was no other reason why any of the family would have been roused, as there were no domestic smoke alarms in those days. The fire brigade were brilliant and attended very quickly with three fire engines; one from Blidworth, one from Nottingham, and one from Mansfield. The house was saved, with the ground floor structurally intact but badly damaged, with smoke damage in the rest of the house.

It was all repaired but for a crack in the glass of a ship's wheel barometer that had been hanging on the lounge wall near the door, an indication as to the heat in the room, and the only remnant of that night. It's still in the family today. Neighbours were very kind. We lived across the road for a while with Mick and Shirley Dunn, until our house was habitable again.

My birth certificate tells me Steve Reginald Cherry was born in the Nottingham General Hospital on 5ᵗʰ August 1960. I've never actually been 'Steven' despite some people thinking I am. My dad, Harold Hector Cherry, born on 16ᵗʰ November 1917, was recorded as a *Colliery Electrician* at Calverton pit, with *Below Ground* written on my birth certificate in brackets, almost as an afterthought, but I can imagine him proudly making this clear to the Registrar. My mother, Lenorah, born on 28ᵗʰ April 1920 did not have an occupation listed. Throughout my childhood she was mainly a housewife but was later a cleaner, working at The Cherry Tree pub in Calverton amongst other things, as though predestined to do it.

My oldest brother, Mick, is fifteen years older than me, and when I turned professional and became known locally, he often told people he was my dad in order to solicit the occasional free pint from football fans, though I'm not sure he'd get away with that today! Pat is my eldest sister, at thirteen years older than me, and then comes Robert or Bob as we called him, the accidental pyromaniac, at ten years older than me. Bob took everyone by surprise right from the start, when my dad was forced to deliver him on the lounge carpet, on his own birthday, so keen was he to come into the world. This eagerness to be early sadly continued to the end as he drank himself to an early death a few years ago. Then there's my sister Lynne who is four years older than me. The age gaps between us all and the fact Bob left home a few years later meant that for most of my childhood we were a family of four.

41 Seely Avenue was a three-bedroom council house, newly built when my mum and dad moved in, and it's still there today, despite our house fire. Both my dad and Mick worked down the local pit, my dad missing the war due to it

being classed as a reserved occupation. He continued there until his retirement when he took £1500 voluntary redundancy when he was sixty-three. One of the biggest reasons he went down the pit in the first place was to help his brother Reg who needed extra funding in order to attend university. He succeeded, thanks to my dad, and went on to become Commissioned Aircrew in the RAF. My middle name Reginald was given in his honour.

My dad was quietly spoken and I never once heard him swear, though my sister Lynne tells me otherwise. When growing up I was often cheeky to my mum, as all lads are on occasion, and she'd say 'Wait till your dad gets home', when I'd face the slipper or sometimes even his belt, but only on the legs, and always in a measured kind of way, never once approaching brutality. It was discipline enforced; my dad had five children in a small house and so corporal punishment was used, but there were never any visible injuries. It was just how it was in those days.

My mum and dad had a very traditional marriage. My mum rarely went out on her own without him, and her life revolved around the house and her family. My mum once confided in my sister Lynne about why there were such huge age gaps between my siblings; she told her that every now and again they would have blazing rows, followed by the usual making up afterwards, with the inevitable result arriving nine months later! They were both hard working and determined people; before I was born they lived at Mansfield Woodhouse, fifteen miles north of Nottingham, and they both cycled to work each day to Nottingham's huge Raleigh Cycle Factory, a journey on very ordinary bikes that must have taken at least an hour and a half each way. There were buses of course, but they couldn't afford the fare every day.

Dad was a lovely man who would help anybody. He was a clever mechanic and would fix people's cars for nothing, but apart from his beer he had just one serious vice: jealousy. He'd often hide in the garage after a night shift in order to catch my mum having an affair with another man, which he never did because she was never unfaithful. He even hid a knife in the side passage of the house just in case, but it never happened. Right up until they were in their seventies he continued his suspicions even thinking my mum might have been seeing the twenty-six-year-old neighbour, Andy, when it was clearly absurd.

My dad loved Norman Wisdom and from my early childhood we'd watch his films together whenever they were on the TV, a passion we shared and continued with right into adulthood. I learned to do some pretty reasonable Norman Wisdom impressions because I knew this would make Dad laugh, particularly Norman Pitkin, the character he always played in his films. I took this further when I'd often entertain team-mates years later by doing the same impressions, which on rare occasions I still allow out of the box today, but only under the right circumstances!

We had some lovely family holidays in the sixties, mainly consisting of my mum and dad and just me and Lynne. We had little or no money, but when you're a kid you've no idea about this of course, you think everyone is the same as you, and so it didn't matter. Dad drove us to Mablethorpe on the Lincolnshire coast in our Austin A40, where we'd spend the day on the beach, and have fish and chips for dinner. Then we'd put the back seat down and the four of us would sleep in the car, in a car park that cost three shillings for all day parking. I don't think we were supposed to stay overnight but nobody bothered us! The car park was close to The Fulbeck pub, where we would use their toilet facilities, and we'd always bump into pitmen and their families whom we knew from Calverton, as everyone went to Mablethorpe or Skegness for their holidays. Dad would play football and cricket with us on the beach; he was a great spin bowler and would give us a brilliant running commentary of every game.

The same Austin A40 was once used to take me to hospital in Nottingham when I collapsed in the school playground. I'd told my mum I felt unwell but she wouldn't listen and insisted I go to school, but I was in incredible pain and it just got worse. I had no idea my mum had followed me to make sure I got there and so when she realised I wasn't joking my dad arrived and they took me in. It turned out to be a grumbling appendix, which they didn't operate on, but just kept me in hospital for a week feeding me *Instant Whip* all day long every day, which was very nice and seemed to cure the problem! On one occasion my dad inherited £100 when his Aunt Martha passed away and so we drove down the A38 to Dawlish Warren in Devon in our red Triumph 1300, stopping for the night halfway at Uncle Reg's house in Swindon.

From my earliest memories football has been a massive part of my life, and very often the biggest part. It's been one of my greatest obsessions right from the start. My first football injury was at the age of two, when I dived for a ball in the lounge and cracked my head on the fire surround, briefly knocking myself out. I saved it though, which was the important thing, and if anyone asks, this could well be my first memorable save. There was a great incentive for that particular save as had it got past me my football would have gone straight into the fire!

When I was five I attended William Lee School in Calverton, where my obsession continued. It was clear even then that I wanted to handle the ball, to save it, to pick it up and kick it, and to throw it; you couldn't do this as an outfield player. Bad weather didn't stop me playing football either; I'd kick the ball around inside the house, throwing it against the living room wall and diving to catch it as it came back at me. I'd move furniture around to give myself more space, and I must have driven my mum mad. I was seven when I dived onto a piece of broken glass on the lounge carpet, probably the remnants of a broken beer bottle, cutting my right knee in the process. It was bad enough for me to be taken to the doctor, but he couldn't find anything other than a small cut, assuring my mother everything was alright. Two weeks later after a particularly forceful tackle at school and to everyone's astonishment a shard of glass an inch long and a quarter of an inch wide popped out my right knee.

I tried unsuccessfully when I was eight to get into the school team as a goalkeeper, but there were two older boys who were better than me, Andy Harper and Gary Hopkins. Andy later had an apprenticeship at Stoke City and went on to be a policeman. When I was ten Andy and Gary left for big school and I was finally offered a place on the team, but as left side midfield. This wasn't what I wanted but I was so desperate to get on the team I accepted. I kept my passion for goalkeeping alive while enjoying playing in the outfield, even scoring a memorable equaliser against Sherbrooke School with my left foot from twenty-five yards out, a left peg kick the power of which just seemed to improve with age. I wonder if the cumulative effects of my dad's slipper had anything to do with it!

Mr Chapman then picked me for goalkeeper after much persuading, and I was deliriously happy; I was in a proper team at last, and as a goalkeeper! My life was complete, and my obsession deepened. The only time I wasn't playing football now was when I was asleep, dreaming about it, or eating. During school lessons I was thinking about football, waiting for the bell so I could run outside to play football. After school and in the holidays my mates and I would organise colossal football games that would run for hours. Seely Avenue was known as the Top Estate because it was the first estate to be built, and we'd play lads from the Bottom Estate, the Park Road East area of Calverton, using bikes or trees as goal posts. Many of these were Geordie lads whose families had migrated south as the pits around Durham closed, so there seemed to be a clear distinction between us. They could be Newcastle United, Sunderland, Middlesbrough or even Durham, while we were Mansfield Town, Notts County, Nottingham Forest or even Derby County. The games would run for three or four hours with twenty or more lads on each side, joining and leaving all the time. There was no referee of course, and no linesmen, order was kept by general consensus and who could shout the loudest. These games developed entirely by word of mouth – there was no Facebook in those days of course – and after a brief pitch-side interview such as, 'Where are you from, Top Estate or Bottom Estate?' arrivals were allocated team places based solely on geography. Occasionally we'd play on a proper pitch with real goalposts on the Pit Field, but we were often chased off by the groundskeeper if he saw us, which of course only added to the fun. The games usually ended when one team finally accepted defeat, and we'd all trudge home exhausted and filthy dirty, but happy. On all but the warmest of summer evenings the air would be filled with the familiar yellow-grey smoke from coal fires drifting up from every house in the village.

2

When I was a kid I wasn't comfortable knowing my dad was watching me play football. This probably seems odd, but I thought that knowing he was there might put me off somehow, or cause me to play worse; I was self-conscious and desperately lacking in confidence. So I asked him not to watch. I regret this now. But when I became a professional player this changed, even though I still asked him to sit where I couldn't see him!

Just before I left junior school our team won the Nottinghamshire Schools Treble – The Six-a-Side Cup, The League Cup, and The League. It was my first taste of success, and it was wonderful. Playing was great of course, but playing and winning was even better. I had no idea at the time that I was very competitive. I assumed everyone wanted to win, all the time, just as I did. I knew my dad was proud of our team successes because I heard him say things like 'Yes I know, my mates told me,' as I would see some of his friends occasionally standing on the touchline watching the games, the dads of the other boys. He never gave me a congratulatory hug, such things weren't done in those days between a father and his son, but I was certain in the knowledge that he was proud of me.

Big school was the Colonel Frank Seely School, also in Calverton. I'd failed the Eleven Plus, which wasn't really surprising, as all I cared about was football. It was a good job I failed because had I passed I would have been sent to Carlton-le-Willows School, where the posh boys didn't play football, only rugby and cricket. I've only ever played rugby once and never really gave it a chance, so who knows what may have happened? I played cricket a few times but – and my apologies to all cricket fans – I was bored very quickly, standing around waiting for something to happen, so again, I don't suppose I ever gave

7

it a chance. You could say as a goalkeeper there are similarities, and I accept that, but I couldn't see it at the time. All my passion and energy was directed at football and I quickly gained a place in the school team as goalkeeper, mainly by natural progression, because I was already becoming known as *Steve Cherry, the goalkeeper.*

Games lessons at my school in the early seventies were often remarkably similar to those in the film *Kes,* with Brian Glover as the PE teacher. Our version, Mr Godfrey, though not completely bald, had a habit of running up to me with the ball and kicking it at me, hard, before running off again. 'What did you do that for sir?' I'd shout, as he replied 'Just testing you lad, just testing.' He loved getting the ball past me and scoring goals and I always found my PE lessons playing football were far too brief before we were back in the classroom, where I would resume gazing out the window dreaming about football again.

Mr Godfrey once had a real telling-off from my mum when he dropped me in the Basford area of Nottingham instead of taking me home after an away game at another school. To be fair I said I was going to visit my auntie Pat near The Fox pub, but she wasn't in, and he didn't wait to find out. I walked all the way home, eventually arriving home very late. My mum also made her presence felt at school when all my kit was stolen from my bag in the school changing room. She was very protective of her youngest child!

In 1971 when I was eleven, there was a school trip to Wembley to watch the England under 19s play Germany. It was in Wembley Arena, near but not inside the famous stadium. Just before we were about to leave after the game I stood with my mate Richard Tomlinson staring up at the famous twin towers almost in a trance. He said to me 'What's up?' I replied: 'I'm going to play football in there one day,' to which he laughed and walked away.

During one RE lesson (Religious Education), the teacher Miss Bryan asked me 'What do you want to do when you leave school?' to which I replied 'I want to be a footballer, Miss,' a comment that was greeted with obvious disdain, along with some chuntering and a visible shaking of the head. But it really was all I wanted to do, and to me there was never any doubt in it, at all. We were twice taken down the local pit right to the bottom of the shaft on familiarity trips, or perhaps careers advice – *this is where you boys will be working when you leave school* – and I hated it. I knew it was not for me; it was dark, claustrophobic, and above all there was no football. My mum and dad knew it too, and I think they were as determined as I was for me to make something of my passion for the game.

When I was fourteen I answered an ad in the local press for a day's goalkeeping course at the Nottingham Forest training ground in West Bridgford, Nottingham, which my mum and dad paid for. Alan Hill was there, Brian Clough's assistant, and two of Forest's goalkeepers at the time, John Middleton and Peter Wells. There were twelve of us lads and I remember from the start Alan being a really nice chap. He was helpful, supportive and very generous with his advice. It wasn't a trial as such and so nothing came of it, and I don't remember expecting anything, but it was a great day that I enjoyed very much. It was my first taste of what the rest of my life could be like in professional football.

I was onto my second paper round in Calverton by this time. I'd started my first a year before but someone had snitched on me to the newsagent that I was officially too young, and so I was sacked after six weeks. It was the first job I was dismissed from and it wasn't a nice feeling. I was now with Pottages Newsagents, and it was when I was on one of these rounds I saw something most people laugh about when I tell them, so I don't tell many; it was about four o'clock one summer afternoon when I had a close encounter with a bright red light in the sky at the end of Seely Avenue. It rose upwards in a brilliant triangular shape the size of three houses, buzzing as it did so, about two hundred yards away from me. I froze, but couldn't stop watching this object climbing higher and faster, as it eventually disappeared beyond Oxton Woods in the near distance. I peddled home as fast as I could to tell my mum. I was relieved to find out my sister Lynne had seen it too, and more; she said she saw not just one but three of them in a triangular formation. It was reported in the local press but whatever it was, I never saw it again.

With my mum and dad's help I applied for a formal trial at Notts County. I was thrilled to be invited down to their training ground in a similar arrangement to the goalkeeping course at Nottingham Forest. With a group of other lads we did some warm-ups followed by some training, and then I played in the second half of a game naively unaware I was being closely scrutinised. I let in three goals and our team lost. They were mainly boys of my own age but some were older and I didn't know any of them. I couldn't shout much goalkeeping advice to them because I was nervous and didn't yet have the self-confidence. I tried really hard but I was aware it wasn't my best performance. I knew I could have done much better. In modern terminology you would call it part of a learning curve, and unsurprisingly, nothing came of it.

Undaunted, I continued playing for the school team, and was approached by The Clifton All Whites, who were connected to Nottingham Forest and

Walsall. They had contacted the school who in turn spoke to my mum and dad. They offered to pick me up from school in Calverton, take me to the games, and drop me back at home. It was an excellent opportunity, and I was lucky to be asked, but I turned it down. Was it a stupid decision? I don't know. I gave my reasons as not wanting to leave my mates, and I also had a fear of being called a bighead. But maybe my failure at the Notts County trial had influenced my decision too.

By this time I was also playing for South Notts under a man called Mr Donnison, and Richard Tomlinson gave me lifts to the games in his car. I'd play for them on Sunday mornings, ten-thirty until twelve, then make sure I was back at Flatts Lane Co-op in Calverton to be picked up to play for another team, Calverton Youth Wing, in the afternoon, changing team kits on the way in the minibus.

My biggest wakeup call in football, however, came from when I started playing for Calverton Colliery men's team when I was still only fifteen. These were fully grown miners, tough blokes who took their football very seriously, and it was probably the best grounding I ever had in football. A good goalkeeper also has to be tough, both physically and mentally; otherwise the other team will literally run rings around you, in between knocking you all over the pitch, so this was excellent experience. A man called Tony O'Brian who lived nearby then invited me to play for Calverton United, which was also a men's team. I was learning the aggression and playing power that was essential in good goalkeeping. In 1975 when playing for Calverton United at Harvey Haddon Stadium in Nottingham, we won 3-2 against Linby Athletic. I made quite a few great saves and was given some wonderful praise from my adult team-mates in addition to that from the spectators. It was my first big game win, and it was fantastic.

My dad kept scrap books of paper cuttings from the very beginning of my career. I'm very glad he did. One of the earliest match reports containing my name is typed on pink paper, like part of a programme sheet, and I've no idea who wrote it:

Today's match was Calverton United v Arnfield FC. This was one of the most boring games it has ever been my misfortune to watch. United were 4-0 up in the first fifteen minutes and were 5-0 up at half time. The second half was a little better and the final score was 8-1.

Despite the report it was an eventful game and a great win for us, even though I didn't have much to do, but the fact it was so one-sided probably made it uninteresting to watch. For me it was memorable because I scored one of our eight goals; the wind was behind us and it was from a goal kick that just kept on going, untouched by anyone else, right into the back of their net a hundred yards away. It's not so much the distance of the kick but the fact the ball passed all their defenders who just stood watching it and then their goalkeeper, who probably couldn't believe what was happening. Little wonder they lost 8-1.

In the same year I played an away game at Ilkeston for Calverton Youth Wing against Ilkeston under 16s. It was an unremarkable game but for the fact we lost 7-1. You might think by this score I'd had a bad time, but it was quite the opposite. We should have lost 16-1 because I'd made nine brilliant saves during that game, probably some of the best in my career. I was catching shots and blocking them really well, not only in diving saves but tipping them over the bar. A goalkeeper doesn't always have a bad game if he loses, because when you make a great save it is incredibly satisfying, and what's more, the crowd know it too. Unknown to me, a Derby County scout called Ernie Roberts was standing near my goal and saw everything. He reported back to Bert Johnson, their chief scout, who then contacted Frank Hill, the Calverton Youth Wing secretary. Soon after that I was invited for a trial at Derby County Schoolboys as a goalkeeper. I couldn't believe it.

3

There's no doubt about it, this could be my big break, and I was very excited. I hoped it wasn't just another experience that might come to nothing, and I knew it could be, so my feet were still very firmly on the ground. My mum and dad were very supportive and we all knew it was a step up from anything else I'd done.

I spent five nights in the Rolls Royce Hotel, Ascot Drive, Derby, with a dozen other lads, and had a great time. Every morning we were given a wonderful breakfast and were picked up by the youth team coach at nine forty-five for the ten minute journey to the famous Raynesway training ground, just off the Derby ring road.

We started with a warm-up, followed by possession football in a square five yards across, with heading, side volleys, passing, and closing down. Of course we'd all been doing this anyway, in our own playing, but it was great to be formally taught the specifics and to understand them so thoroughly. There was a shout across the field for lunch, and we'd all file into the clubhouse, muddy boots off at the door, then hands washed, before hot pies, salads, juices, yoghurts, fruit and cups of tea. There were no energy drinks in those days. We were growing lads and it seemed we were constantly hungry, and I have to say the food was fantastic.

After lunch there was a proper game, played against a team of apprentices. I was only vaguely aware I was being scrutinised, I was too busy enjoying myself and getting stuck in to worry about it. They were great lads and there was a really positive atmosphere around the whole experience. In the evenings we stayed in the hotel on our best behaviour; we knew if there was any trouble it would most likely be the end of any football career before it even began. Dinner was served between six and seven o'clock, all provided free of charge. We each had our own room and the only time I felt a little homesick was at the beginning, on my first night away from home. There was a payphone in the hallway I used every night to update my mum and dad, who were very keen to find out what I was doing. I tried my best and hoped I'd impressed the right people, and when I left with everyone else at the end of the week my future was in their hands, those at the club who would ultimately make the selection decisions. There were only a few who could be taken on, so most would face disappointment.

Two weeks later a letter arrived offering me a post at Derby County Schoolboys, in the Derby County Youth XI. I couldn't believe it. I was elated, as were my mum and dad. I made a point of informing my English teacher at school, Paul Buck, who ran the football team in the evenings. He was chuffed for me, saying 'I knew you could do it, Steve.' It's odd how you never forget those who always had faith in you.

I sat in a huge leather chair with my mum and dad in the Chief Scout's office at the Baseball Ground. Photographs of famous players and managers stared down from the walls all around me, the big stars of football with wide smiling faces holding glittering trophies, all the symbols of success. Because I was quite skinny at the time, when the signing was over Bert Johnson said to my mum and dad with a wry smile, 'The first thing we've got to do is put some weight on him.' I was still only fifteen, a little young to be leaving home. As my mum and dad drove away in their red Triumph 1300 I didn't feel any twinges of loss or home-sickness. This was a dream come true for me. I was to be paid to play football, at £12.50 a week, which doesn't seem a lot now but of course I had no overheads at all.

I moved into digs at 11a Upper Bainbridge Street, Derby, effectively as the lodger to a middle aged couple who did all my cooking and cleaning. I went home at weekends; if it wasn't my mum and dad picking me up it was my sister Lynne, who also used to collect me from away matches. Because I wasn't there two days a week I was given another £10 which I then gave to my mum for weekend board. Unknown to me she saved it, giving it all back to me when I bought my first car. I was too young to drink, I certainly didn't smoke – and never have – and so I saved most of my money. I made some great friends and Steve Ketteridge's parents lived in Stevenage which was a huge distance away so quite often he came home with me at weekends.

One of the first things the club then told us was a few important rules governing our private lives. We were now their potential assets, their investments for the future and so we were to make sure we looked after ourselves at all times: *'No motor-bikes, no skiing, and no horse riding'*. A few of the lads were crushed by the order about no motor-bikes, and I'd only ever been on a horse once when I was seven, when the damned thing threw me off and then bit me, so I didn't go near one again. As for skis; perhaps if I'd mixed with the posh boys at Carlton-le-Willows I may have tried it, but to this day I've never been skiing in my life.

My time was now spent in structured playing and learning about football all day, wearing the number Y33 on my first training kit, with what were now a great bunch of new mates, all doing similar to what we'd done in the week's trial, but with greater intensity. It was a lot of fun too, and the time flew by. Some of the lads became very good friends, such as Paul Bartlett and Steve Ketteridge but others less so. Two brothers, Peter and Keith Falconer couldn't have been more different; Keith was a good player and was a nice lad but Peter had delusions of grandeur despite not being a very good player. What he lacked in talent he made up for in sarcasm, flailing his arms around like an idiot every time I missed the ball, and not in an amusing way. He just wasn't funny. You know the type. Perhaps this was all because he realised deep down that a distinct lack of talent wouldn't take him anywhere in professional football. If it was, he was right, because it didn't.

We all got to know one another well, for better or worse, as you do when you spend so much time together. Colin Chesters used to demand money from anyone willing to watch him pick his blisters and then eat them, at 50p a blister. It was a good earner and he would usually supplement his income by £5 a week, a reasonable sum in those days, in addition to the extra protein he was ingesting of course! He was often loud and aggressive, one of those people you'd avoid if you could. He once threw his chewing gum at me on the coach and it stuck to my hair so badly it had to be cut out, leaving me with a bit missing that was obviously further cause for more piss-taking. He was frequently rude for no reason, and this backfired on him once when physio and trainer Gordon Guthrie caught him sticking two fingers up at him behind his back. Gordon grabbed hold of him and said 'Don't you ever do that to me again!'

When I was training at the Raynesway sometime later, Frank Sheridan ran up to me from twenty yards out and head-butted me on the chin after I'd issued him with some constructive goalkeeper's criticism. My jaw still clicks to this day. I know much of this was lads behaving like lads, I accept that, but some of it was uncalled for and could even nowadays be said to have amounted to bullying, or even assault. It was the way things were in those days though;

no doubt it was the same in other physical occupations, and I know things like this happened down the pit. Sadly we now know much worse has happened to young men and boys taken into training by football clubs. Thankfully I was never a victim of it and I never came across any.

A year later in 1976 I signed a two year apprenticeship contract, again in the Chief Scout's office at the Baseball Ground, with my mum and dad, and the Youth Team Coach Richie Norman. Richie was a nice chap and I'll always be grateful to him for his help and the faith he showed in me right from the very beginning.

In July 1976 during my first year's apprenticeship at Derby County we travelled to Paderborn, in the Rhineland area of Germany, for a Youth Team knockout tournament with a total of eight teams including clubs from Sweden, Austria, and Germany, and one other English club, Southampton. It was my first trip abroad and it was very exciting. Our first game was against FC Vienna, and we drew, 0-0. I was pleased to keep a clean sheet but I think we were the better team. Colin Chesters and Paul Bartlett put them under a lot of pressure and tried a few times to break the scoring but were kept out until the end. I had a fairly quiet game and only had to make one save. We then thrashed the hosts Paderborn 5-1. We were definitely on a roll because the following Saturday we beat Swedish team Malmo 3-0. There was only the semi-final stopping us, so when we beat German team Walsburg 4-0 we were delighted to reach the final, which was ironically against another English team, Southampton, after their crushing defeat of Bayernhof 10-0.

The final was brilliant and I had a great game, keeping out some pretty good attempts, and it ended with me maintaining a clean sheet, winning 1-0. It was my first taste of international football and I loved it, particularly as we'd won the whole tournament, bringing some silverware back to the club.

After the match we began drinking champagne from the trophy as it was passed around the dressing room. Our sponge man Jack Wilmot grabbed it for a quick swig and underestimating its size and weight he promptly knocked one of his own front teeth out, which then plopped into the champagne. Undeterred, he fished it out with his fingers and dropped it into his pocket; we all cheered, laughed, and carried on. There are videos of Jack years later still with a gap in his teeth.

After showering and changing we played darts at a nearby British Army camp, drinking German lager as we did so. It was all free, and I'd never drunk so much before. Someone gave me a whiskey and ginger which I knocked back in one, and after that things became a bit hazy, to say the least. It was decided we'd all go into town on the team bus, apparently to a strip club, and I remember being dragged around and onto the bus by two team-mates. I was still only sixteen and so the prospect of seeing real-life naked ladies gyrating around in front of me was something I was desperate not to miss! Sadly as soon as I boarded the bus I puked up all over the floor and the two front seats (why are there always diced carrots?), and so I was immediately ejected from the bus and never made it into town.

4

The next morning I woke up in some very strange surroundings with little recollection of the night before. I was lying on a wooden bench in a dark cell with grey walls, thick steel bars on the window and a solid steel door, with a smelly toilet in one corner. It was like some bleak fifties Cold War spy film. To my horror the door was locked. What on earth was going on? *Had I killed someone last night?* I shouted and banged my fists on the door but nobody came. What was happening? I shouted again and I heard whistling down the corridor and a rattling of keys, followed by laughter. The door was opened by a big chap in uniform with a bright red face. Apparently I'd been in such a state they'd dropped me in an army cell for my own safety. I had bits of dried sick encrusted all down the front of my shirt, and my black signet ring was missing, but apart from that I felt wonderful. I met up with the rest of the team in the sergeant's mess, all tucking in to a wonderful breakfast.

Not long after Germany, on 28th September 1976 we travelled to Donegal in Ireland for a First Team UEFA Cup match, second leg. The first leg was what you might call a decisive win against the Donegal side, Finn Harps; we won 12-0 at the Baseball Ground. Colin Boulton was on loan to Southampton and the second choice goalkeeper Steve Bowtell was ineligible, so it was down to me. Our manager Dave Mackay had a few words with me in his office earlier that day and told me the experience would do me good, and he was right. The Harps were keen to give us a rematch on home ground and improve on their last performance. We flew to Dublin from East Midlands and stayed at the Ballyraine Hotel in Letterkenny, after crossing through Northern Ireland. At the border our coach was inspected by British soldiers who came on board with their guns. I'd never seen soldiers with guns so close before. There were serious faces all round and a tense atmosphere until one of the soldiers shouted 'Aye up Chaz!' to Charlie George, as though he'd known him all his life.

Letterkenny was a lovely little town on the River Swilly and we were made very welcome. After settling in and a restful night the next afternoon at four o'clock we played Finn Harps at the Ballybofey football ground. It was a much better performance from the Harps and they put one past us, as we only managed four against them this time. I was on the bench for that game and the crowd was going wild and it seemed the whole of Ireland had turned out to support them. It was a good game though, and we all enjoyed it. There wasn't much opportunity for post-match reverie because straight afterwards we were bundled into the coach and taken to Dublin Airport, arriving back at East Midlands at midnight. It was a very quick visit with a lot of arranging just for one game. The goal difference meant we'd still won 16-1 on aggregate.

Throughout 1976 I was getting some very favourable press reports. My dad noticed this more than me and he was always pleased to inform me. He cut them out religiously and stuck them in his scrapbooks, most of which have survived today. In a game where we beat Notts County Schoolboys 2-0 I was mentioned as having 'a good game' and in a 1-1 draw with Northfield Juniors I was described as making 'a courageous save' and 'a number of brilliant saves.' It's not often goalkeepers get noticed, so this was really nice. Of course I didn't know who else was reading these reports, or indeed watching my progress. I didn't get everything all my own way though, I made mistakes and came in for justified criticism occasionally.

In 1977 Dario Gradi was brought into Derby County as a coach and one of the first things he saw us do was lose 4-0 to Ipswich Town at the Baseball Ground, a loss that caused our ignominious exit from the Southern Junior Floodlit Cup. Because it was a defeat you might think I had a terrible game, but I didn't, not altogether. Alan Brazil and Steve Gardner tried all through the first half to get past me and I blocked them twice before they finally got one in just before half-time. The second half was not so good and Noel Parkinson got one past me easily after a free kick from twenty yards. Everyone makes mistakes.

Derby County were being criticised at the time for not producing enough First Team players through their youth system, and were not giving them enough experience in the Central League. It was often left to injuries for some of them to get an opportunity. Dario Gradi knew this and told the *Derby Evening Telegraph* he was busy checking every player, and was quoted at the time as saying, 'One thing I am happy about at reserve and junior levels is that the lads are moving both the ball and themselves about. They are prepared to work things, and try things.' More importantly for me, when asked about Steve Cherry he said, 'He is a very relaxed goalkeeper with a lot of ability and I thought his punching was first class.' At least this second statement made more sense than the first!

In my second year's apprenticeship apart from learning how to clean boots and sweep the changing room I learnt some tricks with a player's most important kit: the boots. 'Stud boots' had studs that were of hard plastic, which were useless on frozen ground, 'moulded boots' were softer, and 'flats' were effectively like training shoes and better for hard ground. The studs were three-tiered, so to gain an advantage we pulled out the bottom sections with pliers, making the stud thinner thereby giving the boot much better grip. These wouldn't have been very pleasant if they ever made contact with flesh, and so of course this was done *after* the referee and linesmen had been into the changing room to check everyone's boots. This didn't only happen in the Reserve team, but in the First Team too, and on match days. I doubt Derby County were the only team to do this, and it's hardly an advantage if everyone does it, but that's how it was then.

It's not all dreary stuff in the changing rooms though; apart from the bar and the manager's office the club revolves around this part of the ground. If you hang around in there long enough you'll be surprised who you might bump into. I had a sweeping brush in my hand the day I realised I was standing right next to the legendary Bill Shankley imparting his knowledge on members of the First Team in his characteristic deep voice, his unmistakable Scottish accent still there. I wanted his autograph, I wanted to talk to him, and I wanted to tell my dad. Sadly I only managed the last of these three.

On 9th April 1977 we played Everton's Youth Team at the Baseball Ground in the FA Youth Cup semi-final. We lost 2-0. I didn't have a very good game and was beaten by a couple of easy shots from Mike Coffey and Joe McBride. None of us on our team played brilliantly. It's odd how that can happen. To be fair, their goalkeeper Nick Banner made a great save from Bob Corrish and so they deserved to win. Everton eventually lost to Crystal Palace in the final, 1-0 on aggregate.

On Monday 2nd May we played Aston Villa Reserves, and lost 1-0. We were unlucky. Andy Crawford and Alan Cork both hit the Villa woodwork before John Capaldi got one past me. Paul Bartlett hit a cracking shot that ended in their side netting. The following Saturday we lost again, this time to Bury Reserves, 2-0. I made two good saves late on in the game, so it could have been much worse. Our bad form continued until we played Preston Reserves, and won 2-0. For us it was an end to a disastrous run of twelve games without a win. To be fair, Preston's goalkeeper Alex Smith made some superb saves, but I kept a couple of good ones out too, particularly one from Ian Cochrane. Brothers Peter and Keith Falconer worked well together to get one of ours and Alan Cork the second.

Playing in the Youth Team and the Reserves was brilliant and I really was enjoying it, but I was still dreaming of a First Team place. A small taste of it came quite unexpectedly in August 1977 when we were at The Den playing Millwall. I was there, as we all were, supporting our team and when our First Team goalkeeper Colin Boulton came off injured close to the end of the game I was ordered onto the pitch as substitute. I couldn't believe it. I was only just seventeen and I was playing in the First Team, and what a place to start!

I was very nervous and my reception from the Millwall fans was predictably hostile but I didn't let them put me off. Within minutes of taking up my position between the sticks, a Phil Summerill header seemed destined for the back of my net when I just managed to tip it over the top to keep the score level at 1-1. When the final whistle blew I was very pleased with my performance and I really enjoyed it. I suppose it was my First Team debut, but I didn't really consider it as such because it was just the last twenty minutes.

Back in the Reserves we then played Shrewsbury in the Midland Intermediate League and lost 4-0, which sounds terrible, but it was another of those games where it could have been much worse. They were on top form when sadly we weren't, it's as simple as that, and I had a very busy time. As a goalkeeper you can tell fairly quickly the way a game might go, and this was one of them. They kept up constant pressure and I could see our defence were all over the place; they got three past me in less than five minutes, but I did well to keep it down to only four!

I must have impressed someone because I was selected to play in a youth team called the Representative XI against Leicester City at Filbert Street on 10th August. I was chuffed to have been chosen but sadly I don't remember much about it, even the score, and I never played for them again.

In September 1977 a new man arrived as manager of Derby County: Tommy Doherty. He'd just come from five years at Manchester United and so his reputation came with him. His expertise was much needed in the Reserves as well as the First Team, because on 10th October we lost 4-1 to Sheffield United Reserves. Again it could have been much worse because I made a few quality saves I was very proud of but there's no doubt we were simply out-played by The Blades. After the game Tommy took me to one side and told me he'd heard good reports about me, and that he thought I had the potential to become a great goalkeeper. I found this incredibly flattering and it really boosted my confidence. This little chat was clearly a deliberate tactic, and it worked. I was only just seventeen so when a manager of Tommy Doherty's stature takes you to one side and tells you he has confidence in you, it can only have one effect. He probably said the same to all the other players but this didn't matter to me. Anyway, something worked because in our next game we beat Birmingham City Reserves 3-1. It may have been coincidence but we all played well. I made a diving one-handed save that I wish had been captured on film.

We then drew 1-1 with West Brom in the FA Youth Cup and went on to lose 1-0 in the replay. Frank Sheridan was sent off in the closing minutes but their goal in the last two minutes was from the penalty spot. Nick Cross was brought down in the penalty area and Phil Danks gave me no chance at all. We had mixed success after that; Stoke City beat us 1-0, and Leeds United beat us 2-1. Thankfully I was getting some fine reporting by national sports reporter Steve Curry, as my dad pointed out, and even when we lost to Leeds he said 'Steve Cherry made a number of superb saves.' When you lose games it's easy to dwell on the failures, particularly as the goalkeeper, because it's you who let in the goals, so you hang on to any shred of compliment.

We played Nottingham Forest twice, with the scores being 1-1 on both occasions. We were evenly matched but in the second game I picked up a painful ankle injury, only just managing to get to the end, hardly able to walk. I'd never been so glad to see the end of a game. Alan Hill, Brian Clough's assistant, could see the pain I was in and very kindly carried me on his back all the way around the pitch and into the dressing room. I doubt he'd be able to do that now! In fact I asked him only a few years ago when I last saw him, and he not so politely declined the offer of giving me another piggy-back ride! It turned out my ankle was quite badly twisted and swollen. I knew I'd be unable to play for the next few weeks because I had this same problem a few times when I was at school.

5

In the eighteen months I lived in digs at Upper Bainbridge Street I saved the huge sum of £500 and was eager to spend it. I took driving lessons as soon as I was seventeen and passed on the second attempt. My first beautiful, fabulous car was a Daytona yellow Ford Escort 1.3. What else would a young man spend his money on in 1977? It was second-hand and cost a fortune at £1,250. The shortfall of £750 came from my mum and dad – with some of the money my mum had saved for me – and a loan they took out for this and my first year's insurance. Everyone remembers their first, and this was no exception. I had a cassette player fitted so I could listen to all my favourite Motown tracks while driving around, and I thought I'd really made it. Of course the biggest thing a car brings is freedom, and so I used it a lot. I had a girlfriend, Julie Griffin, who lived in Nottingham and I used to pick her up from work at the huge Boots factory in Beeston, taking her home to Allendale Avenue in Aspley.

Julie and I met when I was sixteen. A team game had been called off so I travelled into Nottingham on the bus with a mate, Martin Snowdon. He was looking for a new pair of shoes so we called into Brown's shoe shop in the Broadmarsh Shopping Centre, as it was then. Julie was working there and served us. She was gorgeous and I couldn't take my eyes off her. As we left I remember saying to Martin: *'One day I'll marry her.'* I've no idea where that came from. Nothing happened until several weeks later we had another game called off. Julie was still on my mind so I returned to the same shop, alone this time. I stood outside and could see her working, busily chatting to customers and colleagues. I was crushingly shy around girls at the time and so I daren't go inside and speak to her, though of course I dearly wanted to. Instead I sat outside for over five hours, waiting for her to come out. She knew I was there, because later her mate Jo Squires told me. In fact at one point Jo said to her 'Go outside and speak to him, he's been there for hours,' but she didn't. When she finally left the shop I still didn't have the courage to speak to her, as she walked past and onto the nearest escalator. I thought all was lost until she turned and came back down. As she came up to me all I could say was 'Can I walk you to the bus stop?' Luckily she agreed. We then exchanged phone numbers and I rang her as soon as I got home. We arranged to meet in a few days and even on my first date I took a friend, Robert Breffit, with me, just in case, but only the once!

Football was now not the only thing on my mind, at seventeen you can guess what else was, and giving Julie a lift home meant I stood a better chance of getting it when we got there, if parents weren't in and the opportunity was right. I hadn't had the car long when I was negotiating a relatively complex double traffic island on the Nottingham ring road called Raleigh Island and Crown Island when I happened to notice a rather good looking young lady on the footpath to my left. I was trying to see what she looked like in case I knew her, obviously, so I stared at her perhaps a little too long. Meanwhile, unnoticed by me, the car in front had slowed almost to a standstill. You feel a collision before you see it, because if you'd seen it you could have applied the brakes. The noise was horrendous, as such things are; the sudden thud and unmistakable crunching of metal. My beautiful Ford Escort struck the rear of a large silver-gold Mercedes saloon driven by a local businessman and scrap metal dealer, Jack Pownall. He strolled over to me and was surprisingly calm about the whole thing. I was hugely apologetic but it was clear I'd come out the worst as his car appeared virtually undamaged while mine looked as if it had been hit by an express train. I think he took sympathy on me, and didn't raise his voice or even take my details, but just shrugged and drove off. My car was driveable so I continued; picking Julie up from work and dropping her off before I went straight home to my mum and dad's. I didn't know what else to do.

My dad took one look at my car and opened the bonnet. He was murmuring and tutting to himself, and shaking his head, then alternately looking up at me, and then back at the car. I felt terribly guilty. He still didn't say anything before he disappeared into the shed. He had a great mind for mechanical things and every summer when we were kids he'd remove the engine of the Austin A40 and recondition it, before putting it all back in, so he really knew his stuff. Until one summer on the way to the coast it broke down in Lincoln.

I thought for a moment that my dad would come back from his shed with something to batter me with, but he was carrying a massive chain which he then threaded through the engine compartment behind the front grille, anchoring each end around our concrete gateposts. He then jumped into the car and began reversing it up and down the driveway, revving the engine like a madman, causing huge clouds of exhaust fumes to cover the car. By this time a crowd had gathered, wondering why their neighbour, Harry, was using a bright yellow car to destroy his gateposts. Of course dads seem to know instinctively how to fix things. He knew what he was doing. The gateposts remained firm and the massive dent in the front of my car popped out as if by magic. He later slapped on a bit of filler and sprayed it for me until it was as good as new.

Eighteen months into my two year apprenticeship in 1978 I was asked to sign a formal professional contract as an adult with Derby County, thereby securing my place in the Reserves. I'd made it. I could be in the First Team at any time. This was it; I was playing for The Rams. But it didn't feel like it. Even now my feet were still very firmly fixed on the ground. I was given the honour of being a kit man, with responsibility for making sure everyone had the right kit for the right games, and they were all clean and ready. In my first year I had to clean the boots of three First Team players, as was the custom for new lads in those days. Nowadays they employ someone specifically to do this. I used wire brushes on muddy boots and even a touch of white paint was used occasionally to make boots look brand new. I doubt such thrift exists in the top level of football today.

On one of my first outings as kit man for the Reserve Team we travelled to Aylesbury, and the other kit man, my mate Paul Bartlett, had assumed I'd packed the training kit, and I assumed he had, when in reality neither of us had. We therefore had to train in our match kit with our own shirts on top, like kids playing on the park. It was a stupid mistake made through poor communication, and it didn't happen again.

It was around this time that we were warned about fame. Not how good it was, quite the opposite, but how bad it can be when it stops. *People will want to know you when you are famous, and they'll drop you when you aren't.* I heard, but I didn't really listen, mainly because I hadn't experienced anything like it yet.

On Sunday 12th March 1978 we travelled to Syria. I've no idea why Syria was chosen for a few games, but it certainly was an experience I'll never forget, and it's not because of football. They say everyone has a good pooh story at least once in their life, and this would be one of mine. The bus trip down to Heathrow was like a mobile card school, with a huge pile of cash up for grabs in the middle of the bus. In the days before iPads and mobile phones, footballers loved playing cards. The flight with Syrian Arab Airlines was uneventful and even though it was still early spring and close to midnight, Damascus was bloody hot when we arrived.

On the first day we played against a team called Syrian Selection I, and we beat them 2-0, though I didn't play but sat on the subs' bench. I wasn't listed as first choice goalkeeper but I still hoped I'd play. On the Tuesday we spent the day in our hotel, the Meridien Damas Hotel, getting further acclimatised and enjoying the surroundings. The Syrians were bursting with pride when they showed us a pitch that had the most wonderful artificial turf I'd ever seen, before or since. Our second and final game was scheduled for the next day against the Syrian Selection II, and it seemed I would be given the chance to play in at least some of it.

That evening we were taken on a sight-seeing bus trip around the area. I'm not sure what we were supposed to be looking at because by the time the bus set off later than scheduled it was pitch dark. We were driven up into the hills and disembarked to stand looking down across Damascus. It was all very pretty, with the city lights flickering like distant stars in the evening heat. We were then taken back into the city for a formal dinner and civic reception.

We quickly realised the meal was to be in a hotel not two hundred yards from our own. Tired and fed up after spending more than an hour on the bus, a few of the older lads, Charlie George being one of them, sneaked off back to our own hotel. Charlie was already very well-known and an accomplished player having had a great few years with Arsenal before coming to us in 1975. We were all more than a little in awe of him.

I didn't have the nerve to follow. Maybe I was too polite, or too hungry? I think the latter is probably the biggest reason. The meal was superb and very tasty, though I've no idea what it was. There were a few speeches and ripples of polite applause before we all returned across the road to our rooms. It had been very hot in the bus and so I poured a bath to cool down. I felt a bit queasy too, with an increasingly odd stomach ache, and so I hoped a soak would make me feel better. I often wonder what would have happened had I not been in the bath at that moment.

I lifted my backside very slightly in order to release what I thought would be a little underwater trump – as you do – when instead of a few delicate bubbles rippling the surface I suddenly became massively incontinent with an explosion from my bottom the power of which I'd never experienced before, or since, as though Ridley Scott's *Alien* was dropping out my arse. Everything I'd eaten in the last twenty-four hours, or probably my entire life, began pouring into the bath around me, and I couldn't stop it. You've heard the expression 'the bottom fell out of my world,' well in this instance it was similar, but in reverse, as the entire world fell out of my bottom. If that wasn't enough, I was then violently sick with projectile vomiting. In a few seconds the bathwater was a dirty brown mess of pooh and sick and it kept on coming like a broken tap. It was the first time in my life that I'd funnelled from both ends at once and I didn't know what to do.

After a few more violent explosions I stood up, a dripping mess, standing in stinky dark brown vegetable soup. I turned on the shower and rinsed myself down as best I could. I was then sick again into the bath. I didn't know whether to perch my bottom over the bath or the toilet, I was spoilt for choice. Stomach cramps were doubling me up and I kept retching every few seconds. After half an hour of this hell which seemed more like ten years, I dared to crawl across the floor towards the bed, but I was forced back into retreat several times to make more deposits from both ends in the bathroom. Not until my insides were utterly empty did it finally slow down and stop. I continued retching but nothing was coming out.

I was desperately thirsty but daren't drink anything, as it would undoubtedly come straight back up. This is where the danger lies of course, with dehydration. Eventually I climbed up onto the bed which seemed as high as a mountain. I must have passed out because all I remember is our physio Gordon Guthrie standing over me giving me something in the night while mumbling at me as I lay there sweating and burning up. I thought for a moment he was a priest reading me the Last Rites, and for a few delirious moments I was in so much pain I wasn't bothered if he was.

The next morning I couldn't even get out of bed I was so weak. I wasn't too concerned though, I was just thankful to have woken up and found myself still alive. I lay there all day wondering if I'd ever feel well again. Later in the evening, still feeling as fragile as a China doll I trudged down to the restaurant area but I couldn't eat anything. I couldn't even face the sight or smell of food. *'You drink tea, no milk, lots of sugar, okay mister?'* a waiter shouted, smiling at me, standing with Gordon as though they were both taking the piss. I took his advice anyway. The stomach cramps had gone, now replaced by chronic hunger pains, occasionally satiated by cups of sweet tea. It seemed I was the only one to suffer as badly as this.

Our team won the second game 3-0, but the scores had become irrelevant to me, sitting as I was in a wicker chair in the hotel lounge with a blanket over my legs like a ninety-year-old pensioner, the only one to be so incapacitated. The next morning we left early for the nine o'clock flight back to Heathrow. That was my four days in Syria.

6

In the summer of 1978 a letter arrived from the Football Association asking me if I'd like to attend training selection at Lilleshall in Shropshire, for the England Youth Team. Would I? What an honour! I'd been playing well and I'd heard there'd been some very favourable reports about me that were heading in the right direction, so I was thrilled. I travelled in my yellow Ford Escort and it seemed on arrival I was already part of the team. I was measured for a jacket and trousers and was given lots of sponsored goodies including a personal radio. I still have that England blazer today, though it seems to have shrunk a bit in places! The joint managers of the team were Ken Burton and Brian Clough, with Peter Taylor as Brian's assistant. Brian or *Mr Clough* as everyone referred to him, including his own mother probably, was the manager of League Champions Nottingham Forest at the time, and so he was literally at the top of his game. There's a well-known saying that Brian Clough was the best manager England never had. Well he was, albeit in the Youth Team.

I was thrilled to be formally selected for the team and in October 1978 my first trip abroad with the England Youth Team was to Las Palmas in the Canary Islands, in the Atlantico Cup. It was still very hot and most of the team had had a sleep in the afternoon, as we'd all been instructed to do, so we would be fresh for the afternoon game. I shared a room with our other goalkeeper, John Lukic, and that particular afternoon neither of us could sleep so we went for a walk along the beach. To our surprise we came across Dave Butler, our physio, spread out across the sand, sunbathing. 'What are you two doing here?' he said, clearly surprised, and before we could answer him he said 'Get back to your room and get some sleep' as he turned over to make sure he was getting an even suntan.

We walked straight back to the hotel but still couldn't sleep, probably due to all the excitement of the coming game.

Ken warned us that Brian would arrive on the eve of the first game against the hosts, Las Palmas, and that he would most likely pick on someone to ridicule, as he usually did. At four o'clock on the day of the game we were all ready, sitting in the foyer of the hotel waiting for our bus to arrive. It was late. Buses and coaches were pulling up all the time but ours was still missing. It was the hottest part of the day and patience was wearing thin. Just as we thought things couldn't get any worse we all saw Brian coming down the stairs and then making his way in our direction across the polished marble floor. Rob Hindmarsh was first to be rebuked merely for saying hello.

'I want you to smile when you talk to me young man,' Brian said to him, followed by 'and take your hands out of your pockets.'

Please don't sit near me, please I was thinking. Sure enough he sat on my chair arm, right up close to me as though we were best friends.

'Did you get any sleep today young man?' he said, in his typically nasal drawl.

'I didn't actually, Mr Clough.'

'You should have gone for a sleep on the beach, and if you couldn't sleep there you should have told me, you'd have bloody slept then.'

'Yes, Mr Clough,' I said, not knowing what else to say.

When our bus finally arrived twenty minutes late, Brian was chuntering and cursing and began rounding off at a woman who was involved in the organisation of the tour. I could see she was clearly upset and tearful. Eventually she made her way to the front of the bus and began shouting back at Brian, telling him just what she thought of him. 'You shouldn't even be on this bus, there's two too many. It's not my fault it was late and you shouldn't talk to me like that!' None of us players would ever dare speak to Brian Clough in that way and we were all amazed, even more so when he didn't shout back. He didn't do anything. But I did notice from then on he was really nice to her, all the time. It seems if you stand up to a bully they leave you alone, obviously.

Brian Clough told us many times of his way of playing football, which was obviously the best way, and the only way, without question, and at the time it seemed right because he was having so much success. He didn't invite criticism and nobody dare raise their hand to argue football tactics with him anyway!

My first England Cap was on that afternoon, 10th October in Las Palmas when we beat the current European Youth champions, Russia 1-0. I didn't have a lot to do, to be honest, but I made two good saves in the first half and one in the last few minutes of the second. Tommy Doherty was asked about my performance and he said, 'I'm very pleased for him. He has been very patient and deserved this chance.' I didn't know at the time but it was Tommy who had delayed my appearance in the England Youth Team; previous manager Colin Murphy had recommended me to the England squad the year before but when Tommy arrived he put it on hold. Maybe he was right to do so, who knows.

It didn't really sink in at the time that I was playing for my country and what a big issue it was; you just get on with the job and do the best you can. My mum and dad were oozing with pride obviously, particularly when I showed them my England blazer with the famous Three Lions crest, and I was very proud to be part of it. No doubt if it had been Wembley, then things would have been different.

I was chuffed to keep a clean sheet in my first England game, and in the next game when we played Las Palmas we won 3-0. Again, it was a clean sheet for me. I was pleased with my overall performance in Las Palmas but then on November 19th on another foreign trip for England when we played Italy in the Municipal Stadium in Monte Carlo for the Monaco Youth Tournament I let two past me and we lost 2-1. From then on John Lukic of Leeds United played the other games as I sat on the subs' bench.

We had a lot of fun off the pitch too, as young lads will when heaped together for any occasion. We'd been playing in the Mini-World Cup at Villa Park and the entire England Youth Team were staying in a lovely hotel in Birmingham. Most of the team had decided to go out to see a film at a nearby cinema, which didn't appeal to some of us, including me. John Lukic and I shared a room and decided to have some fun with Justin Fashanu, who we knew had also stayed behind. At seven o'clock in the evening we rang Justin's room, a few doors down the corridor. John disguised his voice when Justin answered the phone:

'Hello, is that Mr Fashanu?'

'Yes. Who's this?'

'This is reception downstairs Mr Fashanu. There's a man here who says he's a Spanish football manager Eduardo Garcia, says he's from Real Madrid and wants to talk to you, can I put him on?'

There was the briefest silence. Whether Justin suspected something for a second I'll never know, but he obviously pushed any doubts to one side because he came straight back:

'Yes, please.'

At this point I called on all my imagination, because just like in *Stars in their Eyes* I'd disappeared into the dry ice and re-emerged as Eduardo Garcia, assistant manager of Real Madrid:

'Allo! Allo! Theese iss Eduardo. Ooo ees dis?'

'Hello, it's Justin, Justin Fashanu.'

'Okay, good, 'ow are you?'

'Fine, thank you Mr Garcia, what can I do for you?'

'Iss nice, dee weather 'ere, eh?'

'Yes, yes it is.'

'I am from Madrid.'

'Are you?'

'Yes. Ees nice there too.'

'I should imagine it is, yes.'

'You know it?'

'Yes of course.'

'Madrid, you like Madrid?'

'Yes, I do, very much.'

'*You have been?*' I replied sternly, demanding confirmation. He hesitated.

'No.'

'*So how you say you like it, eh?*' I said, sounding just like Manuel in *Fawlty Towers* rather than anything remotely Spanish. I was half expecting him to realise what was happening, my accent was so preposterous, but he didn't, so I carried on. By this time I looked to see if there was a damp patch on the carpet in case John had started wetting himself he was laughing so much. I thought he was choking.

'Well, I mean it's a great team, and a great city, you know.' Justin replied, in a serious tone, backtracking, as I held out the phone for John to listen in.

'Okay. You want to play for us in Espana?'

'Yes please, that would be great.'

'Okay. You meet me now, okay?' I said, trying desperately to hold it together.

'Where?'

'I am downstairs now, you come down now okay?'

'Yes, of course, Mr Garcia, I'll be straight down.'

Two minutes later we heard a door slam, followed by the padding of feet along the corridor as someone passed our room on the way to the lift. We opened our door and leaned out. Sure enough, Justin was standing at the lift eagerly pressing the call button several times, wearing his best England track suit and looking very smart indeed.

I shouted, 'Justin!'

As he turned to face us John and I both made an appropriate hand gesture towards him. He realised straight away.

7

Derby County Reserves were part of the Central League, which included such teams as Everton, Aston Villa, Wolves, Sheffield Wednesday, Sheffield United and Birmingham City. It was around this time I played Manchester United Reserves at Old Trafford in the FA Youth Cup. We had a good game and were pleasantly surprised to find that we dominated most of the time, despite a very slippery surface. Our skipper Keith Falconer got our first, Mike Quinn the second, and Kevin Murray the third in the last minute, ending the game 3-0. We were really chuffed. I didn't have it all my own way of course, Steve Jones came at me several times and once hit my right post, but it was a pretty weak shot, which he repeated not long after, but this time I came out and smothered it on the ground when he hit it from twelve yards. Attendance was low at 654, but we were still in awe of playing at Old Trafford, one of the biggest football stadiums in Europe.

We then played Nottingham Forest Reserves at the Baseball Ground and didn't do so well. I could sense we might be in for trouble when I made two very testing saves in the first half, one of which was a full length dive. Where was my defence? The pressure was on, and they never let up, with Ian Bowyer getting one past me on the rebound after thirty-seven minutes. With twenty-five minutes left Gary Mills hit a cross into the middle and Stuart Gray headed the ball right past me into the net for 2-0. Sometimes two hands just aren't enough.

You learn quickly not to dwell on defeat, particularly as a goalkeeper, and it very often didn't apply if we'd lost but had a good game. If I'd made some good saves, keeping the score down to a more reasonable level than it could have been, then the loss was easier to accept. You have to work on these positives or your confidence might collapse.

We travelled to The Hawthorns next to play West Brom's Reserves and we had a great game. It often happens like this. Even though we were 1-0 down early on I made some great saves and I had a good rapport with our own defence which kept us in the game. The penalty area is the goalkeeper's domain, he rules it, and commands others on his team in that area and beyond. I now understood that in cross balls and corner kicks it is always much better to stand at the far post, not the near post; it's very difficult to walk backwards between the sticks, much easier to move forwards. We claimed a goal back eventually and the game ended 1-1, which we were pleased with. The Reserve coach Richie Norman was impressed by my playing because he told me, and I know he said so to the manager. It's always nice to get positive feedback.

We then travelled to Goodison Park to meet Everton Reserves. It was yet another famous football ground, one of the places I used to see on the TV and dreamt of visiting when I was a lad, even if now they were virtually empty for the Reserve games. Imre Varadi almost got one past me quite quickly with a close range shot which I deflected over the top for a corner. Then only a few minutes later he came back heading a cross past me into the net which was immediately disallowed due to him being blatantly offside. I'd been criticised in the past for not handling cross balls very well, and I was still working on this. Gerry Daly then got one past their goalkeeper Drew Brand, my opposite at the other end, to put us one up, and then just before half-time Billy Caskey got another past Drew after he'd saved a great shot from Steve Spooner. Varadi was the only one causing me any real problems all through the game but I managed to keep him out and in the last minute Billy Caskey got us another and his second, ending this enjoyable game at 3-0.

We then lost 1-0 to West Brom at The Hawthorns but even though it was a loss I had a good game, stopping several great shots from John Loveridge until Derek Monaghan finally got a low shot past me from the centre. We beat Preston Reserves 1-0 at Deepdale and I had a great game because in order to keep a clean sheet I had to save a penalty. The ball came straight at me. I wondered if Terry Cochrane knew he'd fallen for my bit of professional goalkeeping subterfuge; a tactic I'd started using when I was an apprentice. I've hinted at it a few times to the press over the years but I've never before revealed what it was and how I did it. It's very simple psychology, and I'm not sure where it originally came from, but I'm convinced it works. Prior to any penalty I would stand slightly to the left of centre, or sometimes to the right, very visibly so, making sure the penalty taker was looking at me. I'd even make a noise sometimes and draw his attention to me while I was doing it, if necessary, just to make sure. Why did I do this? Because for a few seconds he sees a bigger gap to his left or right, an empty space where there's no goalkeeper, an easier place to hit the ball, a vast area of unguarded netting. He probably doesn't consciously register it, but he sees it anyway, and hopefully it sticks in his mind. Just before he takes the kick, I'd move back to the centre, ready to dive in the direction of the empty space he's just been looking at. I used this technique all through my career and I'm convinced it helped. I also made a small mark in the middle of the goal line to assist with my angles, which I knew I shouldn't do, but most goalkeepers did the same. I later saved a Kevin Keegan penalty at St. James's Park using this and saved four out of five penalties at Bramhall Lane against Sheffield United when playing for Notts County in the Zenith Data Systems Cup. I believe Paul Cooper at Ipswich did something similar. It doesn't always work of course, this goalkeeper's *Jedi mind trick*, some people for whatever reason are immune to it, but let's face it, it's very lonely standing between the sticks when facing penalties, because you are only too aware the rest of your team and thousands of fans are depending on you, so you try anything that might help.

There were three good goalkeepers in the Derby County Reserves at this time: Colin Boulton, Graham Mosley, who was second choice, and then there was me. Colin picked up an injury and Graham went up to the First Team for a while before eventually going to Southampton on loan, so I became full-time Reserve goalkeeper. It was another step closer to a First Team place. This is very often how it is in the Reserves, constantly on and off, up and down through injury and transfers. It was getting very exciting because I never really knew when I would be called up for a regular place in the First Team.

In 1979 John Middleton was Derby County's First Team goalkeeper, with Dave McKellar as first reserve. Dave was experiencing a loss of form, and so was our manager; Tommy Doherty resigned in May. Colin Addison arrived from West Brom in readiness for the new season. He also informed me I would be ready very soon. I'd be in the First Team any day now.

8

On 22nd December 1979 Julie and I were married. We were living in a rented maisonette in the Beeston Rylands area of Nottingham, close to the Boots factory where she still worked. Things were looking up on the pitch too; First Team goalkeeper John Middleton picked up a shoulder injury and so I made my full First Team debut at the Baseball Ground playing against Southampton, on 16th February 1980 when I was still only nineteen. I'd been on good form in the Reserves in the Central League; in fact we were doing much better than the First Team, so new manager Colin Addison was clearly hoping this would continue, because the First Team were struggling, gaining only two points from the previous eleven games, without a single win in the last twelve, and were sliding down the First Division. There was no Premier League in those days so this was the top league of English football. Adult Standing tickets in the Co-Op Stand 'A' were £2.40. It would be my first entire Division One game between the sticks for Derby County and I was playing against such legends as Alan Ball and my old friend Charlie George, now a Southampton player, and my opposite number was Pete Wells, a fine goalkeeper.

There were 16,000 people in the crowd watching my every move, and TV cameras were there amongst a gaggle of photographers and reporters. It was a huge step up from the few hundred spectators usually in attendance at Reserve games. I was nervous of course, and in my first touches of the ball I kicked it away when perhaps I could have easily picked it up, but no harm was done. I was glad to be busy from then on, facing two corner kicks early on, with Roger Davies clearing the ball away in the second during a goal mouth scramble. I took the ball off Charlie George by kicking it away from him at the edge of the box and then we went on the attack. Pete Wells punched the ball out which

Roger Davies took great advantage of, heading it straight past him into the net. To be fair to Pete he then made a couple of superb saves as we kept up the pressure on him. Alan Ball was booked by the referee for arguing with him and I was busy again as the game moved back into our half. I made a flying one-handed save to keep out a shot from Phil Boyer which I sent over the bar. I was chuffed by this, it was a great confidence boost, and we went into the break 1-0 up.

The second half began well for us, when Aiden McCaffrey headed one over the bar which Pete Wells didn't even get a look at. Only a few minutes later I was punching the ball out of my own goalmouth after a Charlie George corner kick. In the 59ᵗʰ minute Southampton drew level when Dave Watson shot through a crowded goalmouth after a corner. I didn't even get a touch on the ball. I hated it when there were so many bodies milling about in a chaotic mess; it's too easy to lose sight of the ball. Only a few minutes later we went on the attack, with Pete Wells knocking out a shot from Alan Biley, which was then picked up by Barry Powell who rammed it home into the bottom corner of the Southampton net. I don't think Pete even saw it! Only six minutes later a well-timed volley from Graham Baker found the back of my net after I had little chance to stop it. I have to give credit where it's due; it was a good shot.

For a first appearance I had a good game. I didn't make any silly mistakes which I was relieved about, and I think I put in a good performance. I let in two goals but so did Pete, with the game ending 2-2. I was relieved it went well not just for me, but for my dad too, because I knew somewhere in the crowd he'd be sitting there with his flask of *Camp Coffee* and *Brains Faggots* cobs. My brother-in-law Andy Griffin often helped him get to my home games, particularly in the later years, and very often some away games, and I'm very grateful for that.

How does top level football compare to everything I'd done before? It's faster, more physical, and your opponents are less forgiving, that's for sure, as are the crowd. It reminded me of the first time I'd played in the men's team for Calverton Colliery when I was only fifteen; they tried very hard to push me around, both physically and metaphorically, this new goalkeeper, who does he think he is? I was barely twelve stone in 1980 and still only nineteen, but I like to think I kept my nerve. There's no doubt it can be quite daunting going down for a ball knowing there was a real risk of a boot in the head or face, but you just have to accept that, be aware of it, and minimise the risk as best you can. Besides, one of my worst injuries came from an elbow while standing, and not someone's boot.

I was told the first games are the easiest because there's no pressure, no reputation to live up to, and therefore no expectations. That may be true, but the first bit doesn't apply, there is still very definitely a lot of pressure, and the nerves can affect you too. The huge crowd was something I had to get used to, shouting in unison at your every mistake, with a lot of the comments being far from complimentary. Changing ends to stand right in front of the away supporters I felt like Daniel in the lion's den. This was not entirely new but the sheer size and volume of it all certainly was.

My second First Team game was at home again, this time against Tottenham Hotspur, on Saturday 23rd February 1980, again to a packed crowd. We had Roy McFarland back after being suspended at Middlesbrough, and I could tell, because he made a really positive difference in our defence. We were slow starting against Spurs, concentrating more on defence than attack, so our breakthrough didn't come until the 49th minute when Aiden McCaffrey and Dave Langan set up Alan Biley for a header which sent us into half-time at 1-0.

We kept up the pressure after the break, and after only a quarter of an hour Aiden sliced a low shot past my opposite number Mark Kendall into the Spurs net for our second. I then had a clash with Mark Falco in my area which brought him down and caused Spurs to claim a penalty, but these appeals were ignored by the referee, and rightly so, in my opinion. I was trying for the ball and anything else that happened was purely accidental. Roger Davies then missed a chance when his shot flew wide of the Spurs goal. Sadly in the last ten minutes Spurs got one past me; I admit I went out a little too soon towards Ossie Ardiles and Gerry Armstrong passed me while I was still on the ground, leaving an open goal. Tony Galvin's header then flew into the back of my net. I wasn't troubled again though, and in fact I had a generally quiet game after that, thanks mainly to our defence, and it ended 2-1.

I was still thoroughly enjoying playing against such greats as Glen Hoddle, capped many times for England, and Ossie Ardiles, who'd just won the World Cup the previous year with Argentina. Could it get any better? I was living the dream, enjoying life with the big boys in the First Team at the top of English football, I'd been making a great impression, and I was gaining valuable experience. What could possibly go wrong?

Injury: A stupid, careless accident. I picked up an injury that not only kept me out of the First Team but out of playing altogether for a while. The football press stated I'd 'injured an ankle at home' without revealing any of the finer details. You won't believe how it was caused. It wasn't football related but animal related; our kitten Leo had escaped out the front door and I decided to follow him to prevent him from getting crushed under a car, getting lost, eaten by a fox, or otherwise coming to harm. As I ran outside I slipped on the pavement and badly sprained my left ankle as I fell in a heap on the hard ground. So it was not a football injury but an 'animal welfare-related injury,' and probably a first for a Derby County player. No, I'm definitely NOT mentioning sheep at this point!

I immediately knew the extent of my injury because I'd done it so many times before. I should have known, and I should have been more careful. Julie came out to find me sprawled across the pavement, groaning in agony. She thought I was kidding, saying 'Oh just get up Steve,' as she stepped over me with Leo now safe in her arms. But I wasn't messing about. It quickly swelled up and changed to some horrendous shades of black and blue. What a time, and what a way to pick up a serious injury, I was bloody fuming. My first thoughts were the kitten was now safe, but was I?

The next morning I was in such a bad way I could hardly get into a car let alone drive, so Steve Buckley picked me up and gave me a lift to the ground. I was cross with myself and very concerned about my career. I hobbled down the corridors at Derby County like Long John Silver looking for his parrot, hoping to see our legendary physio Gordon Guthrie. I could see in Gordon's face that he was as equally dischuffed as I was. It seemed my glass ankles had struck again. Within five seconds he shrugged and simply said: 'Six weeks.'

9

The following Sunday I missed playing Aston Villa, which was shown live on TV. Dave McKellar took my place. Villa won 1-0. I continued with daily treatment including ice packs and ultrasound, and the best part, great food: salmon sandwiches and tomato soup – still my favourite!

When I returned to full fitness I started back in the Reserves again, easing in gently before playing in the First Team against Manchester City on 24th April 1980, in only my third senior appearance. We were now struggling near the bottom of Division One but Man City weren't doing particularly well either at the time. Even so, our very recent form was good, we'd won our last seven home games, and this game was at the Baseball Ground too, so we were hopeful of a win. Just before the start, our manager Colin Addison formally signed Dave Swindlehurst for £40,000 on the pitch in front of the crowd. City fans were chanting 'What a waste of money!' throughout, amongst other things, but Dave would become a great asset to the club. Prizes and trophies were handed out to young supporters, and Miss Derby County paraded around the pitch looking very pretty, waving and smiling dutifully at the crowd.

The game began well for us after only six minutes when Steve Buckley intercepted a careless ball from Paul Futcher, passing it straight through to Dave Swindlehurst who then booted a glorious shot past their goalkeeper Joe Corrigan from twenty yards. The abusive chanting about him from the Man City fans suddenly stopped! It wasn't such a good start for me because just after that I dropped the ball following a cross; luckily it was kicked out the area in a bit of a mad scramble with no harm done, but it certainly woke me up. Steve Powell brought down Man City's Paul Power just outside my area and I readied myself as Tommy Caton took the free kick, which was a brilliantly powerful ball. Luckily it was wide and flew harmlessly into the crowd behind me to yelps of derision from our fans. Dave Swindlehurst was then taken off with blood pouring from a gash to his eyebrow after a clash with Paul Futcher. A few minutes later Nicky Reid turned the ball carelessly back towards his own goalkeeper which then unexpectedly flew into the Man City net for an own goal; always a goalkeeper's worst nightmare! The Derby fans went into hysterics obviously, and it was a great bonus for us, but I really felt for Joe; after he'd given Nicky a few choice words of advice I could see he was totally deflated.

Dave Swindlehurst came back on after twenty minutes with two emergency stitches in his brow, desperate not to miss the game. Just as I was thinking Joe Corrigan was having more of a busy time dealing with several corner kicks, the action came my way when I deflected a shot from Kaz Deyna, the Polish International, which hit my left post low down. Seconds later I then punched the ball safely away after he made another attempt. Dennis Tueart then kicked the ball over my crossbar, which I like to think I could have got a touch to if it had been any lower. When a ball comes at you high, you can instinctively tell whether it's going over the top, or at least you hope it is, but those that eventually hit the bar are a different matter. You must try to get a touch, just in case. Much of this comes from experience, obviously, and from those endless hours of training while standing between the sticks.

At the other end, Alan Biley headed the ball over their crossbar and was keeping up the pressure when he was needlessly brought down by Paul Futcher just inside the box. Joe Corrigan did well to get a touch to the ball in the resulting penalty, but it still went in, taking us 3-0 up at half-time. Our fans were going wild.

After the break Man City were a different team. Their manager Malcolm Allison must have threatened them all with the sack, and I can imagine the spittle flying around between his expletives. Whatever he said to them it worked, because we hardly got a touch on the ball let alone any shots on their goal, and I was kept very busy. I went on to make some of the best saves of my career: A full diving save stopped a shot from Ray Ranson and then another from Dennis Tueart. Whenever I got the ball I kicked it as far as I could down the field hoping I'd never see it again, but still they kept attacking. The Man City fans were getting louder as I stopped yet another good effort from Dennis Tueart, and then a great shot from Steve McKenzie, which I knocked over the top at full stretch for a corner. I shouted at our defence, trying to muster them together, but the inevitable happened when Dennis finally got one past me from a corner kick in the 82nd minute. We then had eight minutes and a few agonising extra ones for injury time to keep them out, which we did, the game finally ending 3-1. What a fantastic game. We were ecstatic, as were our fans. I was exhausted.

At the final whistle a lot of Derby fans stormed the pitch with some even climbing into the directors' box shouting 'We'll support you ever more!' Luckily the directors had managed a quick exit beforehand, some of them visibly running for cover as though they knew what was coming. There were no boos or jeers, even though it looked like we were facing relegation. Colin Addison was quoted in the *Derby Evening Telegraph* as saying 'You've never seen a team drop into the Second Division with a crowd like that. If the season lasted another four games we'd be out of it.' He was probably right; we'd been on great form that day. I was chuffed to be voted Man of the Match; it was just what I needed on my first game back.

I was then massively disappointed when the club signed goalkeeper Roger Jones from Stoke City and also Yugoslav goalkeeper Yakka Banovic from Australian club Heidelberg and I was back in the Reserves. Employing two or three good goalkeepers is obviously very sensible in case of injury, and it keeps them all on their toes if done correctly, but for me this was like a kick in the teeth as Roger kept his first team place from then on and played really well, eventually winning Player of the Year from the fans. As a consolation, I travelled with all the lads to Magaluf for a team break. There was no formal training, and the booze flowed in limitless amounts. I had my eyes opened as to the off duty lifestyle of some professional footballers. It must have been something about being a footballer that some people found had very powerful aphrodisiac qualities.

In the spring of that year I also began training for the *Ramathon* half marathon with my brother. I've never been particularly interested in running as a pastime, and only did it to keep fit, but Robert wanted to do it, so I went along with him. He smoked and drank a lot, so perhaps I was hoping it would get him fit. He was also an asthmatic. We ran a mile first, then three miles, and then eventually ten. We ran from my mum and dad's in Seely Avenue, Calverton, down Main Street, past Ramsdale Golf Club, left onto the A614, left onto Dorket Head, left down Bank Hill into Woodborough, and then left back into Calverton along Main Street. I was so pleased with our achievement I had it placed in the next Match Day Magazine. This was a mistake. When manager Roy McFarland saw it he ordered me into his office, without telling me why. He wore his stern face like a banner for all to see and was clearly upset about something, but I couldn't think what it was. I hadn't been late for work and I was performing well in training and on the pitch, so I was utterly clueless.

He stood three feet in front of me, looked me in the eye and said: 'Rest days are for resting, not running fucking marathons you twat. Don't do that again.' I was shocked, but relieved it was only that. He was right of course. I could easily fall and shatter one of my increasingly famous glass ankles. 'I should fine you a week's wages but I won't because you're playing well at the moment, but take this as a warning, okay?' he said to me. I left his office suitably admonished. As it turned out I missed the race I was training for anyway because it was the week I was away in Magaluf with the team.

I played in our last game of the season at Carrow Road against Norwich City on 2nd May. It was very windy right from the start, and I kept the ball out early after two quick corners, with Justin Fashanu causing me some serious problems. He was probably still thinking about his telephone conversation with Real Madrid's assistant manager Eduardo Garcia! Dave Swindlehurst took the game back to them, but he miss-kicked a near open goal, missing a great opportunity. Not long after that I kept out a Martin Peters close range header, which was still dangerous when Justin headed it again, but this time it went harmlessly over the bar. Martin kicked a shot wide from a corner and after yet another corner I went too far out to challenge Keith Robson because he then kicked the ball low and fast, right past me into the net after hitting the post first. It was a mistake by me, I admit, but Keith was lucky the ball spun back into the net rather than rebounding away, as it could so easily have done. We then missed a couple of chances before half-time when a Keith Osgood header flew wide, then Gerry Daly took a shot across the Norwich goal which had beaten their goalkeeper Roger Hansbury and would have gone in if it had been on target, but it missed. At half-time we were only 1-0 down, so we were still in with a chance.

I was busy almost straight away in the second half when I knocked a chip from Kevin Bond over the bar with one hand. Justin Fashanu kept up the pressure on me, and now he seemed to have the wind behind him he was even more dangerous. It's obvious the ball has greater speed with the wind behind it, and this is exploited to the fullest, but it can also cause the ball to be less predictable too, particularly in the longer shots. It's just more information a goalkeeper has to bear in mind while standing between the sticks.

I kept the ball out after a corner only to then find Justin lingering briefly unmarked near the far post from where he headed the ball downwards and into my net for their second. I could have sworn he shouted 'How do you like that Mr Garcia?' as he ran down the pitch, celebrating, but I can't be sure!

When you're 2-0 down you can either curl up and hope for the final whistle, or use it as a prompt to play better. We tried the latter. Dave Swindlehurst gained us a corner from which Aiden McCaffrey scored from just outside the box. Suddenly we were back in the game and our fans were fantastic in their support. Sadly our goal only seemed to reinvigorate the Norwich players too, and Graham Paddon kicked a blinder from ten yards that I didn't even touch. While we were still mourning this third goal and feeling pretty sorry for ourselves Norwich attacked straight away, hitting the post from the edge of the box, the ball running over the line and into the net after I mistakenly thought it was going wide. Alan Biley then added to our misery by missing an open Norwich goal from only ten yards, but we kept up the pressure and Dave Swindlehurst eventually got one back just before the whistle, ending the game 4-2. From a spectator's point of view, more particularly from a Norwich City fan's point of view, it was a good game. I was reasonably pleased with my own performance, but it showed how weak our defence was becoming, despite almost losing my voice I shouted at them so much. I enjoyed the game though, and it was good football, but it was a sad reflection of our overall loss of form, and in the summer of 1980 we faced the inevitable: Relegation.

10

Our first game in Division Two was on 16th August 1980. We lost 3-0 to Cambridge United. Not a very good start. We made up for this four days later when we easily beat struggling Chelsea 4-2, followed by a win of 2-1 at Luton. Sadly after that we had only thirteen wins in the next forty-three games of that season. Most were draws, but even so, not particularly inspiring. In October 1980 I picked up yet another ankle injury and when I could walk again and start training in November I was sent on loan to Fourth Division Port Vale in Burslem, Stoke-on-Trent, where their manager John McGrath had no hesitation in signing me up, initially for just a month. Sending players out on loan is common practice amongst most clubs, as you probably know, particularly when injuries are involved; it can help ease them gently back into full fitness.

Port Vale's first choice goalkeeper, Mark Harrison, had a bad knee and was in a worse condition than me, and so it was my opportunity to get back into the game with less pressure. Mark's girlfriend at the time was TV celebrity Fiona Philips, and with my wife Julie we began socialising together as two couples, and they were great company. Unbelievably Mark had been the Southampton goalkeeper when we played against each other at Paderborn in Germany. Not only that, I was Nottingham born and started at Derby, when Mark was Derby born and had started at Nottingham Forest.

Because it was a much smaller club Port Vale inevitably had a different atmosphere, with everyone mixing more and knowing one another better than at a big First Division club like Derby County. I played in four League games and four FA Cup games for Port Vale, the most memorable of which was an FA Cup game on 13th December 1980 against Burnley at Turf Moor. Mark was still injured so I was more than happy to step in. It was a tough game and I worked

45

hard to keep them out, making quite a few really good saves until it ended with a 1-1 draw. The whole team played well and it was fantastic when we carried this on by beating Burnley 2-0 in the second round three days later.

I really enjoyed my time at Port Vale and learned a lot from it. Any time spent learning is therefore never wasted, but after three months I was relieved my injury had fully healed.

When I returned to Derby County things seemed to have changed, and it was not just because they were settled in the Second Division. For me personally there was no noticeable difference from playing in the First Division, it didn't worry me much, though I think it did some of the other players. What a team doesn't want after relegation is a flight of good players from the club, like rats leaping from a sinking ship. We were all aware of this and at the start of the season everyone had worked particularly hard but it clearly wasn't enough. The winter of 1980/81 was becoming pretty tough for Derby County.

I played more games in the Reserves and the 'A' team and hoped I'd impressed the right people with my fitness and great form. Yakka Banovic and I had been bumbling around for months and for the first time I had my doubts about my future with Derby. But how could I leave? They'd been great to me, and it's where I was given my first big break. I decided that at least for now I'd put such thoughts to the back of my mind. As I shared Central League duties with Yakka I gripped my lucky rabbit's foot ever harder and just got on with it. What else could I do? I was still being paid after all.

Just when it seemed the bottom might fall out of my world it very nearly did. On September 5th in the beginning of the 1981/82 season I was in goal against Leeds United Reserves at the Baseball Ground, when after a particularly physical clash with a Leeds player my shorts disintegrated and ripped right down the back in an instant and dropped to my ankles. It was a good job I wasn't playing commando style or it would have been a case of *The Wind in the Willows*, with everything hanging out. Nothing like that had ever happened to me before, and not since, thankfully! There's a photo of it somewhere.

Fate always comes knocking; all you need to do is know when to answer the door. Roger picked up an injury and to my surprise Yakka was placed on the 'available' list in the Autumn Sales. Yes, we have sales at football clubs, but they are not like the ones you know at the shops! It wasn't long before that there were rumours I was to be sold for £20,000 in order to raise some cash, and Yakka was to stay as Roger's number two. It's a fickle business. Between you and me, Yakka was highly rated when he arrived, but didn't quite live up to expectations. This made me number one again, and so Colin Addison picked me as first choice for a game against Bolton Wanderers on 23rd September 1981. We lost 2-0. I blame our defence, and the pace of the game, much faster than in the Reserves. Not good enough excuses I know, and so I was desperate to prove I could do better. My next game at Charlton Athletic on 3rd October was an improvement, despite losing 2-1 I had a much better time; another of those occasions where even though we lost, I put in a good performance and the score could have been much worse.

It was around this time I received a very odd threatening letter. Any mail addressed to players at the club in those days was distributed by Gordon Guthrie who placed it on the player's towels in the dressing room on match days; mine was under the No.1 peg. Players would probably receive half a dozen letters a week, mainly from fans asking for autographs which most of us were happy to oblige with, through the club. This one looked different from the start because my name was typed in capital letters on a plain white envelope, looking very formal. There was one sheet of paper inside which simply read, again in capitals: MAKE SURE YOU LOSE TODAY OR YOU'LL BE SHOT. SIGNED: THE IRA. I was stunned. For some reason I looked around the room while holding the letter in my hand. Why me? No-one else had one. I had no connection to anyone in any such group of people. I handed the letter to Colin who advised me to ignore it. I don't even remember which game it was or whether we won or lost, but I obviously wasn't shot. It was still worrying though, and it was passed on to the police, but I didn't hear anything more about it, apart from later that night. The TV news announced that another player, Callum O'Hanlon of Rotherham United, had received a similar threat. For a moment I wondered why I wasn't mentioned, but I was glad.

Our slide in performance continued, as did our attendance figures. We lost 3-2 to West Ham on 7th October 1981 in the League Cup, and 3-0 to Newcastle Utd on 10th October. As a team we weren't playing well and the club's financial problems worsened, with rumours we were now over a million pounds in the red, which was a huge sum in those days.

1982 didn't start well either as we lost 3-1 to Bolton Wanderers in the FA Cup on 2nd January, and from then on until the end of that season we won only six games. Perhaps we'd do better next season? We had a new manager, as John Newman arrived at the club on 25th January with high hopes and lots of great new ideas, as all gaffers do when they first arrive. John was a nice chap, a gentleman, and I got on well with him from the start. He was extremely knowledgeable about football and we developed a good working relationship based on mutual respect.

In the summer of 1982 Julie and I made our first of many subsequent visits to Menorca and Majorca. I love the Balearic Islands and it was on one such visit to Alcudia in Majorca I was involved in a very odd football game with some locals. I'd been playing in a friendly and very informal kick-about five-a-side game at the hotel when I was invited to gather a full eleven-a-side team together for a more formal game against the Spanish hotel staff. Amazingly enough an ex-Nottingham Forest player Gordon Coleman was there as was Graham Fearn who used to play for Derby County, and so we agreed.

We drove our rental cars a few miles to a nasty looking dirt pitch where there was a huge pot of sangria waiting for use after the game. It all looked very promising. Because I was captain, manager, and sponge man of our team I decided on positions, putting a tall chap in our goal so I could play up front for a change. It was like being a kid again on the Pit Field at Calverton, except for the heat and dust. The Spanish were laughing and very confident, finding it all very amusing; they'd apparently done this many times before and had never lost a game. The sangria was obviously for their post-match victory celebrations.

The first ten minutes were friendly enough, until we scored a goal, and then the Spanish smiles melted away like ice-cream in the sun. After our second goal the kicking started, gradually at first and almost imperceptibly, until it became all too obvious. I'm surprised my leg wasn't broken I took a knock that was so violent and completely unconnected with the game; I didn't even have possession at the time. This should have been a warning. Just before half-time I got our third goal with a lovely chip straight over their goalkeeper's head. This was clearly the signal for the punching to start. Graham took a blow to the face that was so severe I was surprised it didn't floor him and knock him out. Other players on our team were being surrounded and the punches really began to fly. Where was the ball? No-one knew. It had become irrelevant as it turned into an all-out scrap on the dirt pitch. Seconds later I decided it must be half-time and so I signalled our team and we were all of the same opinion: let's get out of here! So while pretending to gather for a team talk we ran for the cars to make a quick exit similar to the footballers in the film *Escape to Victory*, which then rapidly turned into another well-known film, *The Italian Job*, as our three hire cars tore across Alcudia line astern just like in the film.

Safely back at the hotel no-one was badly hurt and we hit the bar and the beer for a hilarious debrief. We felt and looked more like rugby players after a tough eighty minutes. Astonishingly there was no animosity from the losing staff later, as it seemed the worst offenders were from another hotel. It was an interesting game, to say the least, even if it only lasted forty-five minutes. I wonder if I can class it as another England cap and a victory for my country?

We met some lovely people on our regular visits to Menorca. On one occasion I'd just shaved off my moustache and we shared a taxi from the airport with a couple who said 'We were supposed to be sharing this with Steve Cherry the Derby County goalkeeper' not realising I was sitting right next to him. Alan and Shirley Hickling became good friends, as did Pat and Terry Thomas from Essex. It's important to have friends unconnected to the workplace in order to maintain a different perspective on life, and this applies to any profession.

Sadly the 1982/83 season also began badly for Derby County, with three successive losses to Carlisle United, Halifax Town, and QPR, before our first points on 8th September, with a 1-0 win over Chelsea. It's hard to believe now that Chelsea were a poor team at the time, struggling even to stay in the Second Division. On 6th October we beat Hartlepool United 2-0 in the League Cup, but then it would be another *eleven games* before our next win. In October as we slipped further down the table there were rumours about John Newman's position, even though he'd only been at the club nine months. He was juggling the team around trying to find the winning combination like moving the deck chairs on the Titanic in the hope it wouldn't sink. We then had a disastrous 4-0 defeat to Leicester City on 23rd October. For the Hartlepool rematch at Victoria Park he dropped midfielder Brian Attley and winger Paul Emson, and significantly for me he also dropped Vjekoslav Banovic, the goalkeeper, in favour of me.

I suspected I'd be busy, and I was. After only eight minutes I blocked a shot from Roy Hogan which was then picked up by Micky Barker who mercilessly took advantage of my position to get one past me that I didn't even get a chance at. Twenty minutes later Kevin Wilson equalised with a great shot from twenty-five yards out, keeping us in the game. But then just before half-time Trevor Smith lobbed a long shot over my head which I thought was way off target but to my horror bounced straight into my net.

The second half was more of the same. I stopped a shot from Kevin Johnson but Paul Staff picked up the rebound and booted it so hard I thought it might rip a hole in my net. Later on I saved a header from Kevin Johnson that I was proud of just as the game entered extra time. We managed a second goal when Mick Brolly knocked it in from a Dave Swindlehurst cross, but Kevin Johnson never gave up, getting their fourth past me in a goalmouth scramble, never my favourite. I kept out a point-blank shot from Paul Staff and the game ended 4-2 to Hartlepool. Luckily we were still in the Cup due to our previous win, so on aggregate the score was 4-4.

Five days later we were at Molineux playing Wolverhampton Wanderers. We were playing well until a controversial penalty just before half-time, when my psychology didn't work on Geoff Palmer. Andy Gray then got one past me in the 54th minute, but undaunted John McAlle put a great shot past my opposite John Burridge to keep us in the game. Even though it ended 2-1 to Wolves we played well as a team, with a definite improvement. Both Mick Brolly and Kevin Wilson had several shots at the Wolves goal and George Foster and Steve Powell played really well in defence. I kept a few out from Mel Eaves, Wayne Clarke and Andy Gray. It was a good all round team performance, despite losing. It's not great to lose, nobody likes it, but if you play well it's not so bad, and the fans know this too. Feedback from fans is absolutely crucial; a team is nothing without the fans. Sadly there weren't many to see this performance, as the overall attendance at Molineux that day was less than 4,000.

On the 6th November we travelled to Hillsborough. By this time we were close to the bottom of the table and rumours about John Newman's job were never ending and at the forefront of everyone's mind, and constantly in the media. It's the wrong sort of distraction for a team, and really doesn't help. To make things worse for us, Sheffield Wednesday were doing well near the top of the table, so their fans had high expectations against 'struggling Derby' as we were now known, but we were determined not to give them an easy ride.

We had a good history at Hillsborough with more wins than losses, if that actually has any influence, and we started well when my opposite number Bob Bolder had to dive full length to stop a ball from Ian Dalziel in only the first few minutes. Not long after that it was my turn to perform as I kept out a great shot from Kevin Taylor and then Dave Mills sent the ball wide after a twenty-five yard free kick in a busy few minutes for me. To my surprise the Derby fans and even some Wednesday fans stood up to applaud this flurry of goalkeeping, and I was really chuffed by this. Goalkeepers hardly ever come in for any praise so it was great to get some from the most important people in the game, the fans.

I then blocked a header from Mick Lyons as Wednesday kept up the pressure before Ian Dalziel and Gary Mills took it back to them. Gary was unlucky when one of his shots missed the Wednesday goal by just a few inches. Quickly back in our half I then blocked a determined shot by Andy McCulloch and a Mick Lyons shot flew safely over the bar.

It was 0-0 at half-time and we were given a standing ovation and applause from our fans, while the Wednesday team walked dolefully to the dressing room to whistles and cat-calls from theirs. For the first few minutes of the second half we dominated the game and my opposite Bob Bolder was busy with persistent shots from Kevin Wilson, Mick Brolly and Ian Dalziel. Then disaster struck when Steve Powell brought down Gary Megson in my penalty area. There was no doubt about it, he seemed to be aiming at the man as well as the ball, and so for the second week running I faced a crucial penalty.

Gary Bannister placed the ball on the spot, ignoring all my hints as he walked calmly back a few yards, not looking at me once until he booted it into the back of my net without me even getting a touch to it. Gary was obviously on a roll because just before the end he got another one past me, ending the game 2-0. Despite the loss, we played well, though it was becoming all too regular and poor consolation to the fans, our current knack of playing well but losing. The very next day, on 7th November 1982 under significant pressure John Newman resigned.

11

We couldn't have Peter Taylor as our manager because he'd retired in May that year. Or could we? There were rumours flying around, sightings, hushed conversations, and so it was a welcome sight but not a total surprise when Peter emerged from retirement in November 1982 to become our manager. We were all saddened to see John go, obviously, but chuffed to see Peter.

Bolton Wanderers were our first opponents under the new management, on 13th November. I had a pretty quiet game and so did my opposite number Seamus McDonagh as very few chances were created by either side. Bolton Wanderers were also struggling and inspiration was sadly lacking across the entire pitch. Attendances at the Baseball Ground were slipping further, and the figure for that game was a lowly 11,000, a sad reflection considering the glory days' record of 42,000 for a Spurs match in 1969 under Brian Clough.

The following week we took on Oldham Athletic, also at home. Peter Taylor had brought Archie Gemmill and Brian Attley back into the team, with both Andy Hill and Glen Skivington dropped.

Oldham had won their previous five games, whereas we hadn't had a victory in our last nine. We knew we must work harder and with this in mind we began well. Mick Brolly, Dave Swindlehurst and Ian Dalziel kept my opposite Andy Goram busy for a while until I had to make a diving save to stop Darren McDonough. Twenty minutes into the game Paul Heaton took a corner for Oldham which Jon Bowden headed on to Rodger Wilde who cleverly tapped it past me with a very neat header which I admit I completely missed. We went on the attack after that, but Rodger Wilde's booking minutes later for a nasty challenge on me was typical of this game, with quite a few being brought down and free kicks flying around all over the place. Several players needed treatment on the pitch for minor injuries, keeping the sponge men of both teams busy. Despite playing well, we went into half-time still 1-0 down.

Peter was quite generous with us in the dressing room, with few of us coming in for much direct criticism. Perhaps he was still getting to know us, while making less than subtle hints to Archie and the others up front that they could improve their game. Consequently we had a good start in the second half, with Dave Swindlehurst quickly getting a low shot past Andy Goram for our equaliser. Archie Gemmill, Ian Dalziel and Mick Brolly kept up the pressure on Bolton and our fans were fantastic in their support, until eventually in the 73rd minute Ian chipped the ball wide of Andy Goram and into the net to go 2-1 up. A few minutes later Mick Brolly was unlucky when his shot hit the bar, and then I was subjected to every goalkeeper's nightmare, an own goal. John Ryan was closing in and dangerous when Mick Brolly lost him, and Ryan took a shot which George Foster tried to clear but he miskicked it, sending it straight behind me into our net. The reason it's a nightmare of course is that you never expect it from one of your own, and so there's really not much you can do about it, unless it's right in front of you, which this wasn't. Having said that, it was a good game; ending 2-2 with the attendance at the Baseball Ground a little higher at almost 12,000. So there were some modest signs of improvement all round. We hadn't lost anyway, which was the important thing.

We then drew 1-1 with Burnley, won 3-0 at Rotherham, lost 2-1 to Fulham and drew 1-1 with Crystal Palace. The game on 27th December against Newcastle United was memorable for me because it was a minor personal triumph; it was the game in which I saved a penalty from the legendary Kevin Keegan. I'd been following Kevin's career, capped for England numerous times and European Footballer of the Year twice, so he was huge. Not only that, I was surrounded by Geordies in St James's Park, reminiscent of the Bottom Estate Geordies at Calverton Pit Field, but with a massive attendance of 30,000. I'd been getting more than a little gentle ribbing from them all through the game too, that is until I saved Kevin's penalty; I turned and gave them a big smile, which wasn't reciprocated, obviously. There was no doubt he expected to get the ball past me and he was clearly surprised when he didn't, as were the Newcastle fans. I used my full psychology on him, briefly leaving one half of the goal wide open for him to see before he took the kick, right-footed, which I anticipated correctly and stopped with one hand. The Newcastle fans were downright hostile after that, but to be fair some of them clapped, but not many. It sent our fans into hysterics.

We'd been reduced to ten men after Ian Dalziel had been sent off for some heavy tackles after the referee's patience finally ran out, and this was indicative of the nature of this game, where tempers were running high. It's odd but you can just tell when a level of animosity occurs between teams that's more than the usual and this was one of those occasions. We were doing well right up to the 65th minute boosted by Kevin's failure and my save, until Howard Gayle, on loan from Liverpool, got one past me. I was really annoyed, having managed to keep Kevin out from the spot, to then give away an easy goal like this. Kevin didn't give up either, making two more good attempts which I kept out, holding the final score to 1-0. I was pleased with my performance that day and will never forget saving Kevin's penalty.

In addition to Steve Buckley I became great mates with other members of the team such as Bobby Davison and Kevin Wilson. The four of us would often drive out to various pubs in and around Derby, sharing the driving. When it was my turn we'd all pile into my green and black Ford Capri, and I know Capris are considered fabulous classic cars nowadays, and for the most part they are, but mine was awful; the gearbox was unpredictable at best and the vinyl roof was hideous, but apart from that it was great! We found a fantastic pub called The Blue Ball at Risley, which between ourselves became affectionately known as *The Frozen Knacker*, where we'd play pool and drink Double Diamond. Then we'd call in at Steve's place in Sandiacre where he had a pool table and continue the games. Steve acquired the nickname Bagatelle Bill, which he still answers to today, in the right company, but don't tell anyone! Our pool games became so well-known that the latest winner proudly announced his victory when we all returned to the club, because if not we would all be asked anyway.

1983 began quite well for Derby County with a 2-2 draw against Oldham Athletic on New Year's Day. On 3rd of January we took on Queen's Park Rangers on our home turf. We felt different as a team, better, more motivated, and it showed in our playing. We'd gained our second goal before I was even required to do some work, making three saves in quick succession from headers by Bob Hazell and Tony Sealy. Gary Mills got one past my opposite Pete Hucker, before Dave Swindlehurst did the same from a Mick Brolly free kick. It was a scrappy game at times with some odd decisions by the referee Bert Newsome; on one occasion Bobby Davison was clearly deliberately pushed by Bob Hazell in the penalty area but play was waved on. To some in the 14,000 crowd it was a good decision, obviously, but to others it wasn't. At 2-0 it was a very welcome win for us. After the game Peter Taylor gave the press some real gems of football manager philosophy, one of them being: 'I said last week that we had a lot going for us behind the scenes and the only thing missing was a few wins.' Quite so, Peter.

To say Derby County games against Nottingham Forest are important is a huge understatement. There is massive rivalry between the two clubs as though they are opposing teams from the same city, rather than thirty miles apart with the M1 motorway in the middle. These matches are often called *the East Midlands derby* and perhaps the rivalry is so fierce because they are often evenly matched. Some say much of it is about which club has greater claim to the Brian Clough legend, as he managed both clubs successfully in his time, winning them both the First Division titles. Indeed, every time the two now meet, since 2007, the winner receives The Brian Clough Trophy in memory of the man so influential to both clubs. Derby County are the current holders, having beaten Forest 2-0 at Pride Park on 15th October 2017.

Forest fans call Derby fans 'sheep shaggers' and in return the Derby fans would say 'you're only jealous 'cos you've got no dicks and can't shag anything'. And so it goes. Nice friendly rivalry! Local reporter David Stapleton managed to get several quotes from me about this forthcoming game for the *Nottingham Evening Post* on 6th January: 'There can't be a better tie in the round. It's great being a local lad; certainly it's my own special match,' followed by: 'Now that Peter Shilton is no longer with Forest the people I respect most are John Robertson and Garry Birtles. Both are so gifted.' I'm trying to remember now whether I really meant that or if it was just something I said! There was also some bitter rivalry between the managers too; Peter wasn't speaking to Brian at the time, apparently, and so this added to the bitter atmosphere between the two clubs.

I also mentioned in the press that I had eight family members travelling to the Baseball Ground for the forthcoming game, and I'm wondering now who that would have been; my mum and dad, certainly, my sister Lynne and her husband Roger, Andy and Kate Griffin (Julie's brother and his wife), and probably Marie Griffin and Patricia Griffin.

So, on 8th January 1983 we hosted Forest at the Baseball Ground in the FA Cup. Brian Clough was still the Forest manager at the time. I've always loved the FA Cup, as most players do. It's great to get the opportunity to play teams you wouldn't normally meet, both the little teams and the big boys. Forest decided not to play Colin Todd, after he was expected to, with Ian Bowyer replacing him in left back. Todd was one of our ex-defenders, which was another issue between the two clubs, the relatively high incidence of player swapping between them. It was bound to happen due to the geographical location making it attractive to the players on a personal level.

The atmosphere was buzzing with excitement as we kicked off towards the Normanton End, and I could see – and hear – the area of terracing reserved for Forest fans was absolutely packed and a sea of red and white. They certainly let us know they were there. It started with a general kick-about to get warmed up but then quite early on Forest were granted a free kick just ten yards outside my area, which thankfully was wasted when Mark Proctor booted it high straight over the bar. My opposite, Steve Sutton, then took a knock from Andy Hill which required a bit of on the pitch treatment. I knew Steve well and had a lot of respect for him. He saved a couple of good shots before it was my turn to keep one out from Mark Proctor. Then the referee George Courtney stopped the game in order to speak to a linesman who was apparently having things thrown at him by Forest fans, probably money, which happens surprisingly often. He then walked off the pitch into the tunnel to inform the police, while we stood around waiting.

When play resumed Steve Hodge was booked for a foul on Kevin Wilson, the free kick from which was booted away by Gary Birtles. There was a lot of intense play between Forest players John Robertson, Gary Birtles, and Kenny Swain, with ex-Forest player Gary Mills making life difficult for them, which made entertaining football, and the score remained 0-0 at half-time. The Forest fans saw Gary Mills as a traitor of course, and let him know this at every opportunity!

We were pretty evenly matched at the start of the second half too with very few chances at goal from either end until Kevin Wilson was brought down by Willie Young just outside the Forest penalty area. Archie Gemmill then got our first from the resulting free kick in the 63rd minute. The home supporters were going mad, and for us it was a fantastic atmosphere. In the last twenty minutes Archie Gemmill limped off injured to a standing ovation from Derby fans, and was replaced by Ian Dalziel. We kept up the pressure on Forest until the 89th minute when Andy Hill beat Steve Sutton to get our second, with the game ending 2-0. I was very pleased I'd kept a clean sheet.

There is definitely something special when these two teams play one another.

This was reflected in the attendance that day at the Baseball Ground at 28,000, and record receipts of £72,000, a nice little earner. I'm sure Nottingham Forest could play Derby County every month and they'd still get high attendance figures at each game.

12

We thought we were on a roll after beating Forest so decisively. But football is a harsh mistress. Despite playing well, and feeling like we were an all-round better team, we were still haunted by further relegation as we slowly drifted further down Division Two. As any football manager will tell you, winning games is the most important thing in football and not just treading water with draws all the time.

We were then kicked in the teeth when we travelled north to be decisively trounced 3-0 by Carlisle United. We hoped for better things when we then hosted Leeds on 22nd January. Peter brought back my mate Steve Buckley and also Kevin Wilson, but as soon as the game began I was busy right from the first whistle. My opposite number that day was John Lukic, my mate from the England Youth Team days. I was pleased he'd made it as I had into top level football, as he should, he was an excellent goalkeeper. I was the first to concede a goal when Arthur Graham's powerful shot after ten minutes left me standing. There are shots like that sometimes. Quite often I suspect a ball is kicked so hard and contains so much kinetic energy that even if I took hold of it I would be knocked into the back of the net with it.

Only a few minutes later I saved an Eddie Gray header from an Arthur Graham cross before we finally went on the attack, but to his credit John was playing really well and kept everything out. I had a flurry of three corners to deal with, knocking a shot from Frank Gray over the bar before we went into the break still at 1-0 down.

After the usual dressing room home losers team talk it took only a few minutes until we equalised thanks to Bobby Davison. But then four minutes later Leeds gained the lead again when Paul Hart chipped the ball over my head and into the net, after I hoped it would clear the bar but didn't. John Lukic was then forced to make a great diving save that I would have been proud of, from a Gary Mills shot, but then only minutes later as Arthur Graham stood briefly unmarked near my far post he chipped in a cross from Eddie Gray to get Leeds's third. This was a real blow but you can allow these things to deflate or inflate, depending on your own attitude as a team. We were kept in the game in the 63rd minute when we were given a free kick which Dave Swindlehurst smashed into the Leeds net, decisively beating John despite his best efforts. John was unlucky to then face a penalty from Archie Gemmill, which beat him quite easily, with the game finally ending 3-3. What a game. I really enjoyed it.

By now we'd settled down to a routine with Peter Taylor, and understood his way of doing things. Every Friday morning we'd all meet in the boardroom for a pre-match discussion about the team, our tactics, our fitness, our strengths and weaknesses and who we were facing the next day. The state of our pitch was often discussed. The Baseball Ground was one of the best grounds but sadly had the worst pitch. It was okay at the beginning of every season but it quickly deteriorated into something resembling the Russian Front. Lines were drawn across mud rather than grass and near the end God only knows how referees and linesmen could make out where they were. Was it a drainage problem in the grass? There was so much sand thrown onto it as the season went on in a continual effort to dry it out that we nick-named it The Beach. One of the good things about it though was the fact the cinder track around the pitch was very narrow, so you really felt much closer to the fans.

Peter used to walk into the team meetings with Roy McFarland his assistant, and single someone out for particular attention. For a while it was Mick Brolly. 'Mick, I can make you a better player but I can't make you better looking, you ugly bastard,' he'd say, as everyone laughed, with some spitting out their tea. But it was embarrassing, and it was the same every week until Mick began sitting further back as though trying to hide. Sadly it wasn't enough; he'd still get picked on. Eventually he sat right up against the wall next to the window with a curtain draped over his face and entire upper half of his body, with just his legs showing. This made it even funnier of course, but not to Mick. This treatment seemed very unfair because he was a great player and what's worse was he wasn't even ugly! Not as such, anyway. It eventually stopped when Peter turned his attentions to someone else. To our collective shame none of us said anything, how could we? Peter was the gaffer. There was a very strong chance if anyone had objected they would have been dropped from the First Team; such was the power of the manager. But I should have said something, particularly after what happened to me in my early days as an apprentice. But we were all glad as individuals it wasn't directed at us. It's odd, and it's wrong of course. Perhaps Peter had picked up the habit from Brian Clough who was a master at it. It's not the best way to motivate a team by isolating one of them, and certainly not the best way to motivate one team member in particular. Perhaps they think it creates fear and therefore respect? It creates just as much resentment and unhappiness too, which is presumably not what they want. Good leaders inspire their staff they don't create fear. I remember when Darren Fletcher was starting out as a reporter he caught Brian Clough in the tunnel before a game and said 'Hi Brian, can I have an interview after the match?' causing Darren to be ignored for three hours until he finally got his interview, all for not addressing him as 'Mr Clough.'

Peter would do other odd things like taking us all to the cinema in Derby to see 'Gorky Park'. I'm not sure this would happen today. He also took us on a day trip to Scarborough for a paddle in the sea. He said the salt water would be good for our feet, but the North Sea was bloody freezing. I was the only member of the team to dip my feet in the water. I didn't mind. It reminded me of our wonderful family trips to Skegness when I was a kid. In the evening the team visited some of the local pubs and one night when sharing a room with Steve Buckley after we'd all had quite a few beers I apparently tried to get into bed with him. I find this very unlikely. He's not my type for a start! It seemed I was sleep-walking and he finally had to wake me up when I thought his bedside cabinet was a toilet.

I asked Peter if I could visit my hero Peter Shilton and get some training with him, and he said he'd ask for me. I heard nothing so I asked Peter again, this time when he was in his office. He picked up the phone and apparently spoke to someone at Southampton where Peter was at the time before putting the phone down within a few seconds saying 'You can't. They're away. Is there anything else?' Needless to say it never happened. Peter Taylor was a good enough manager, but he was a much better assistant manager. I had huge respect for him but I wondered if sometimes he was just a little out of his depth. He brought some of Brian Clough's worst managerial attributes and tried applying them himself, and he wasn't very good at it.

We desperately needed a win to stop the slide, but our next game was an FA Cup match, against Chelsea. At the time Chelsea were also struggling in the second division, and were playing so badly they were actually below us in the table.

We started well with a goal from a great header by Kevin Wilson in the 18th minute. Chelsea were then given a corner and Mickey Droy was causing me problems until Gary Mills helped me out with a back pass to me, so I booted it as far as I could down the pitch. It came back almost immediately, with Mick Brolly and Gary Mills forced to work really hard in defence to keep it away. My opposite, Steve Francis, did well to stop Kevin Wilson, grabbing the ball at his feet, and moments later it was back with me, so I kicked it safely away from Dave Speedie who was lingering dangerously just outside my area. I had one more touch on the ball before we went into half-time 1-0 ahead.

When the game resumed I dealt with two corners in quick succession by punching the ball away as Chelsea pushed on with their attack, boosted by the roar from 5,000 of their travelling fans. They kept up the pressure until rewarded in the 79th minute when Colin Lee came down the right and found an unmarked Mike Fillery who side-footed the ball past me into the net for their equaliser. Kevin Wilson and Mick Brolly took it straight back to them and Kevin got his second past Steve Francis before the final whistle went at 2-1. The Baseball Ground was in uproar. It had been a very lively game and very vocal crowd of 23,000 but they were praised by the teams and the police for their good behaviour, as there wasn't any crowd trouble at all.

Only a week later on 5th February we played Chelsea again, this time it was a league game, at a bitterly cold Stamford Bridge. Outfield players can run around to keep warm, whereas goalkeepers have to jog around on their little piece of turf between the sticks doing stretches and leg raises and so on. It can get pretty cold standing there in January and February; I wore a cotton t-shirt underneath my goalkeepers top, and tracksuit bottoms tucked into my socks. However cold it became you couldn't wear any more clothing than this, as it would then begin to restrict movement, which could be disastrous. You might stand there all toasty and warm in ten layers of clothing looking like *The Michelin Man*, but you wouldn't be able to save any goals! Better to be a bit chilly. Besides, I've never actually played in a game as goalkeeper where I had absolutely *nothing* to do for the whole ninety minutes. Even if the ball is not in your half you must keep a constant eye on play because literally at any moment it could be right there in front of you.

I'm pleased to say we beat Chelsea 3-1 in our first away win of the season. Of our three goals one was an Archie Gemmill penalty, and one was an own goal (from a miskick by John Bumstead), with Gary Mills getting the first after only three minutes. Colin Pates got one past me, which I was obviously annoyed about, but it was a welcome win for us, and we generally played well, with Paul Futcher now back with us from Oldham Athletic. I have to say Chelsea were not brilliant, and this was reflected in the attendance figures that day, at less than 9,000. Perhaps it was the cold? I certainly remember how very cold it was. It's hard to believe now that Chelsea were once such a struggling team.

13

My life was pretty intense at this time; I was in my early twenties and totally dedicated to my career. I knew little else other than football, and apart from playing some golf in my spare time most of my energies were directed at football, and rightly so. This was after all what I'd always wanted.

I'm often asked 'What was your best game?' There's no easy answer to this as I've enjoyed so many, the majority in fact (and you tend to forget the worst ones!), so how would I pick just one? It's just too difficult, but there are a few that are up there in the top ten. Could the decision be based on how well I played, how many saves I made, the quality of the saves, or just how memorable the game was? Who makes the decision anyway, is it just down to me, the fans, colleagues, or sports reporters? If you remember what I said earlier about a great game not necessarily resulting in a win, then you'll understand why to me, one of my best performances of my entire thirty-year career was on Saturday 19th February 1983.

It was the fifth round of the FA Cup and Derby County were hosting Ron Atkinson's Manchester United at the Baseball Ground. They were near the top of the league and were on great form, so good in fact that they went on to win the FA Cup that season. We were not expected to win, in fact United were tipped to have an easy time at the Baseball Ground. Perhaps this helped, going into a game as the underdog, with few people expecting a great result? None of us were going to allow them an easy time though, that's for sure, least of all me. We had a capacity crowd of 34,000 crammed in with not an empty space anywhere, and the atmosphere beat even the recent Forest match. United had apparently brought 11,000 of their fans, of which their deafening noise was clear proof.

Only a few minutes into the game I was busy; Man United's Steve Coppell delivered the ball to the centre and right in front of me which Steve Powell could have intercepted and made safe but he slipped and missed it, leaving me dangerously exposed. At that point I considered going further out, and the idea flashed through my mind in an instant, but I stayed where I was, a split-second decision that I hoped would be the correct one. The ball was in the air in front of me and placed perfectly for Frank Stapleton to head it towards my net, a classic set-piece that I anticipated; I dived high and to my left and managed to get a fingertip touch on the ball at full stretch, just enough to keep it out. I was really chuffed I stopped it, and this first save of the game really boosted my confidence, as an early save often does, and up until then it was probably one of the best I'd ever made in front of such a large crowd.

It's always great to make a highly visible demonstration so early on because everyone around you then knows what you are capable of. They knew then that it wouldn't be easy to get past me.

I then stopped a powerful shot from Norman Whiteside, the rebound from which was thankfully sent clear by Steve Buckley. The game was in our half most of the time until this point and we just couldn't get it away. Steve Coppell came close again and his pass to the centre was knocked away by Steve Buckley for a corner. When this was cleared a few minutes later we were granted a free kick just inside United's half after Gordon McQueen was judged to have obstructed Andy Hill. Archie Gemmill took the kick, passing it to Steve Buckley down the left hand side, who then ran in for a shot at goal which was easily caught by my opposite Gary Bailey. The ball briefly stayed in their half and we looked dangerous for a while before they came back at us. Norman Whiteside ran up for another strike which I intercepted but it rolled out of my hands to Frank Stapleton who then took a chance and booted it, but thankfully it flew wide. The game carried on at a similar pace, rarely slowing down as United kept up their attack. John Barton cleared the ball off the line with a header while standing right next to me following a corner, after which there was yet another corner kick. Bryan Robson had a shot which I stopped amid a throng of players before the half-time whistle blew at 0-0. I was exhausted.

The half-time team talk was restrained. I was praised for my work between the sticks and we were all delighted to have so far denied United, but we were definitely not complacent. The main thing was we weren't losing, and so there was no shouting and swearing in the dressing room. If you are losing at home at half-time there'd be angry recriminations and some generic insults from the manager without always naming the targets. It wasn't necessary. If the defence had been weak it only took 'We can't keep on (*insert appropriate expletive here*) defending like this, it was (*insert second expletive here*) rubbish…' and so on, to realise who was being reprimanded. If we were losing away at half-time there was a little more sympathy. If I'd made a silly mistake I might get a 'Chez, what the fuck are you doing?' or similar. But managers are acutely aware you can't knock a goalkeeper's confidence too much, it could make things worse, so it would usually stop there. Managers were always in the dressing room. I've seen full cups of tea flying across the room and bits of kit thrown around and kicked about in temper from various managers.

Soon after the whistle resumed play Arthur Albiston took a shot which I stopped, then Steve Coppell tried with a very powerful low shot from close in which I also stopped. Steve's face was a picture; I don't think he could believe I'd saved it. I was earning my pay that's for sure. This was how this game was for me most of the time, stopping shots one after the other in a game in which I was almost constantly busy, more like a training session than a proper game. As time went on we were daring to hope we might earn the replay we wanted when disaster struck. In the 85th minute Steve Coppell passed to Norman Whiteside who ran forward to position himself just in front of my penalty spot, quite close in, for a moment finding only me in his way. There was nowhere else he could go, I was totally exposed. He kicked the ball past me to my right and into the net leaving me slumped forward on my knees. I was devastated.

Several more corners followed before Andy Hill gave us hope by winning us a corner in return. We knew a win was out of the question so all we really needed now was an equaliser to give us the replay, but this corner was held safely by Gary Bailey with no problem. At the final whistle we felt utterly dejected, but this was eased by the fact we'd played so well, even though we lost 1-0. Everyone was exhausted too, and saddened by the fact this meant we were now out of the FA Cup.

I came in for some great praise for my performance from both managers and the press, which I was obviously very pleased about. Reporter Vince Wilson called me 'Sizzling Steve' and 'Man of the Match,' a fantastic accolade for a game against Manchester United. It featured in *Match of the Day* on the BBC and the late, great Jimmy Hill said of my playing 'A most accomplished exhibition of the art of goalkeeping,' with Bob Wilson then adding 'He was brilliant wasn't he?' These were truly humbling comments and high praise indeed from a great goalkeeper such as Bob.

There's no doubt this game has stuck in my memory for the sheer number of saves I made, and the quality of most of them. The Baseball Ground took a massive £108,000 in gate receipts that day, a new record, of which we players took a small share. I made money from another source that day too; after the game I collected quite a haul of coins thrown onto the pitch near me by Manchester United fans, all or most of which were probably aimed at me. I had a full handful which I dropped into a young lad's hands near the tunnel on my way off the pitch, shouting 'Here, there's some pocket money for you, thanks to the Man United fans.' A friend of mine, Tony Grahame, quite by chance recently heard this incident being discussed by the lad himself, now a man of course. His name is Steve Hollyoak. I'm amazed he remembered it, but I suppose it was quite unexpected. Throwing coins is a dangerous and idiotic thing to do, but once done it was nice to make someone happy from it.

14

Winning is obviously the best way to revive a team's spirits following a loss, and so we were on the lookout for one, urgently. Our next League game was on 26th February when we faced visitors Grimsby Town at the Baseball Ground. They were fifth in the table and therefore above us at the time, and so a win might not be easy. Dave Swindlehurst and Archie Gemmill tried really hard, Archie hitting the post on one occasion, but my opposite, Nigel Batch, despite being busy kept a clean sheet as I did, and so the score was 0-0 at half-time. There was no comparison with the Man United game though, in any respect, something I noticed straight away. The game seemed so much slower with neither side threatening the other very much, in quite a contrast from the week before.

The second half moved a little better and Nigel Batch made a fine save after a header from Kevin Wilson. There's no animosity across the pitch at another goalkeeper if he makes a great save. You don't wish he'd drop it or trip up because you know exactly how he feels; you are experiencing exactly the same fears and stresses as he is. As a goalkeeper you can spot silly mistakes though, and for these there isn't a lot of sympathy.

In the 55th minute we were gifted a goal when the ball glanced off Grimsby's Kevin Moore straight past Nigel Batch and into his own goal, as I said, always a nightmare for any goalkeeper, and Nigel had my sympathy for that one. Two minutes later we got our second goal ourselves, thanks to a Mick Brolly pass to Bobby Davison who headed it into their net. Grimsby fought back, and I had to stop a great shot from Kevin Drinkell, the Second Division's leading goal scorer at the time and a shot from Tony Ford, followed by a fantastic Joe Waters effort which hit my right post, but the game finally ended with a 2-0 victory for us.

The rest of the season wasn't too bad; eight draws, five wins, and only two losses. Our last game of the season on 14th May 1983 was against Fulham at the Baseball Ground. Fulham were at the top and hoping for promotion, while we were at the bottom, desperately trying to stay clear of further relegation. It was a memorable game but not for the quality of the playing or the score line. The first half was uneventful and it was 0-0 at half-time. Not long into the second half Mick Brolly headed a beautiful cross to Bobby Davison who booted the ball with his right foot straight into the top left hand corner of the Fulham net in what was a fantastic goal. My opposite, Gerry Paton, didn't stand much chance to be fair. This could have dashed Fulham's hopes of promotion; meanwhile our fans started chanting 'we're staying up staying up staying up!'

Then there was the main reason it was memorable: the fans began climbing onto the pitch, slowly and in small numbers at first, and only up to the touchline, but all around the ground. Police dogs were brought on at the opposite end to me and it was kept under control for a while, but as time went on more began standing around the touchline as we continued playing. After I caught a long shot from Tony Gale a fan ran out from behind and patted me on the back, giving me the shock of my life. I turned around and to my astonishment I saw my goal was entirely surrounded by people. I couldn't believe it. Was I back on Pit Field at Calverton? Ray Houghton then took a long shot at my goal which I just got a touch to at full height in what was a pretty good save, under the circumstances, giving Fulham a corner. By this time everywhere you looked fans were on the pitch, standing around the touchline, now ten deep.

The Fulham manager Malcolm MacDonald was on his feet protesting and I have to say it all seemed ridiculous. You can see it for yourself if you look it up on *YouTube*. At one point I saw my glove bag being taken off the pitch by one of the fans, so I ran after it, actually leaving my goal unoccupied while play was at the other end. I managed to retrieve it and threw it into the back of my net. Minutes later Ray Houghton took another long shot which I tapped over the bar and again another fan ran up behind me, and patted me quite vigorously on the back saying '*Well done Steve!*' The Fulham player who then took the corner had to push his way through the crowd to get to the corner post, it was that ridiculous. Another Fulham player, Robert Wilson, was then tackled by a fan who kicked him on the leg, and then one minute eighteen seconds from the end the referee blew his whistle for offside. The rest of the 21,000 crowd thought it was full-time so they all ran onto the pitch, swamping everyone. Fulham player Jeff Hopkins was punched and had his shirt literally ripped off his back, leaving him quite badly shaken. The game was then abandoned. It had been too stupid for words and potentially dangerous for both players and fans. Despite official appeals by Malcolm MacDonald and later offers by the Derby County Chairman Mike Watterson to hold a replay the result stood. It was the oddest professional game I've ever played in, and must be the only one that lasted eighty-eight and a half minutes!

If anyone asks me I always say the 1982/83 season was my best year at Derby County. It was my busiest, my most dedicated, and most successful. This was reflected in the fact I won Player of the Year at an awards ceremony in May 1983, which is made more special because it's voted for by the fans themselves. Archie Gemmill had been tipped for it and I suspect he was expecting it, so it was a lovely surprise and an honour when it came my way. I'd gone from third choice goalkeeper in the 'A' team, and even briefly on the transfer list, to Player of the Year in just eighteen months. At the awards ceremony Peter Taylor said 'If Peter Shilton came on the market tomorrow, I would turn him down.' Nothing to do with the fact that Derby County were struggling financially of course, but it was still the greatest tribute to be compared to my all-time hero. He also said I was 'one of Derby's many nice guys,' which I thought was good of him to say. As I stood holding the trophy for my acceptance speech I made reference to the support I'd received: 'This award is not for me but for my wife, my parents, my family and my close friends. I would like to thank the other players and the supporters who have been unbelievable.' I said this with genuine sincerity and it was fantastic to be able to publicly thank the important people in my life.

The 1983/84 season began on 27th August with a game against Chelsea on our return visit to Stamford Bridge. We'd not met since February when we'd beaten them twice in quick succession, and they hadn't forgotten this. They were absolutely determined to avenge this score line history and there was a lot of pre-match build up in the media about it. They certainly made sure they did it too, putting five past me that day; Nigel Spackman in only the 4th minute, Clive Walker in the 52nd minute, Chris Hutchings in the 54th minute, and then Kerry Dixon got two, one in the 62nd minute and the last just before the end in the 88th minute. The game finished 5-0, in an ignominious defeat and a sound thrashing for us, the perfect revenge for Chelsea in front of their home crowd of 17,000. I made some good saves but I just couldn't keep them out, and our defence was sadly lacking, as was our goal scoring! It was our worst possible start.

Two days later we faced Sheffield Wednesday on our home turf. I knew I had to bounce back and regain my confidence as soon as possible. It was a scrappy start with three fouls and three off-sides in the first few minutes. We were still hurting from being so badly mauled by Chelsea, and were trying desperately to shake it off but we were not doing very well. John Roberston was trying hard but I was forced to save a point-blank shot early on from Gary Bannister, the deflection from which luckily hit the post and went out rather than in. But we went into the break in the lead after a John Roberston cross found Bobby Davison who did well to get the ball past my opposite Bob Bolder and into the net.

Wednesday must have had an inspirational half-time team talk because they equalised after only two minutes when Gary Bannister smashed the ball past me into the net with a low shot just after a free kick. Wednesday could clearly smell blood and sent on Imre Varadi who caused me a lot of problems until Paul Futcher was judged to have fouled him in my penalty area in a particularly strong tackle. To my horror I then faced a penalty shot, the taker being Gary Megson, and it was only ten minutes from the end.

I lingered for a few seconds over to one side, the way I do, making sure Gary could see me as he placed the ball on the spot. I may even have nodded at him a little, pointing at the open goal, inviting him to aim for the biggest gap. He ran up and took it. It worked a treat. It may have been coincidence but I dived exactly the right way, knocking the ball fifty yards clear. I had to make two more saves before the game ended 1-1. We'd certainly played better than at Stamford Bridge, but we were still generally uninspiring, and only 10,000 had come to see us. Some of that low number was obviously connected to the fact the terraces were still closed following the pitch invasion on 14th May, our punishment from the FA, soon to come to an end. Sadly Paul Futcher, back from Oldham at the beginning of the year, and Bobby Campbell, recently signed from Bradford City, were not making much impact. To be fair, Steve Powell picked up a dislocated elbow during the match and Steve Buckley was injured with a thigh strain, so we weren't having a lot of luck. Our next game was a rare win, 2-1 against Swansea, with Bobby Campbell and Bobby Davison the scorers. It would be our first and last win for *eight games*.

We beat Swansea City 2-1 on 3rd September, and then lost 1-0 to Brighton and then a disastrous 5-1 to Blackburn Rovers. When we faced Oldham Athletic on 17th September at home I was desperate to make a good impression, always vital after such a bad drubbing in a previous game. Oldham had lost their previous four games so they were looking for a win too. We started really well when Bobby Campbell beat my opposite Andy Goram in the 20th minute sending us one up. There was then a flurry of activity in my penalty area when Oldham appealed for a penalty after Dick Pratley appeared to handball while on the ground, an appeal that was thankfully ignored by the referee. But then Paul Hooks' back pass to me was intercepted by Joe McBride and I had to dive at his feet to get hold of the ball. There's always a risk of getting a boot in the face from doing this, and it does happen, but you just have to put it out of your mind for a moment. Ten minutes later Bobby Campbell got our second from a pass by Bobby Davison, which would surely win us the game.

But I could see Oldham were not going to give up that easily. Roger Palmer took a shot at my goal which hit the bar, and he continued battling away until a few minutes before half-time he beat me with a header, sending us into the break at 2-1.

Roger Palmer resumed with determination until he struck again, beating me in a goal which was thankfully deemed offside. Oldham kept up the pressure until a Joe McBride header gave them the equaliser. I made several more quality saves I was proud of which kept us in the game, and we created three more chances at a goal, but the most obvious area that was lacking was our defence, again. As a goalkeeper you can tell when your own defence is poor because you keep on seeing opposition players coming at you with the ball, unmarked and free to take a shot. It sounds obvious but it's true. Why weren't they being challenged and the ball taken from them? The game finished at 2-2 but we could so easily have won.

15

On 7th October 1983 I appeared in a double-page centre spread in *The Ram,* Derby County's monthly club newspaper, talking balls for some of the time; that is the difference between the new Dunlop and the Mitre. I said I preferred the new Dunlop because I could kick it further, even though some colleagues stated it didn't play as well as the Mitre. There were definitely some subtle differences between them, but from my point of view it was the first time some people were noticing just how far I could kick the ball!

There were various photos in the *Ram* article of me in different poses; on the sofa at home with Julie and two of my England Youth Caps, holding both our cats Leo and Felix, with a spade in my hand in the garden, a paint roller, a hoover (with Julie on the sofa in the background clearly in hysterics), one of me watching TV, and one with a golf club in my hand. All great public relations stuff. There was also one of me standing with Peter Taylor when I received the Player of the Year Trophy. I was quoted as saying I love housework and decorating. There's more than a little artistic licence there, as anyone who knows me can tell you my DIY skills are not brilliant. I can paint walls, change a light bulb and a plug, and I'm good at emptying cat litter trays, but that's about it. But I did enjoy golf, and it was my new passion which I still enjoy today. I made reference to the five goals Simon Garner of Blackburn Rovers put past me on 10th September and the fact goalkeepers can't dwell on such things for long, which of course is true. You have to shrug them off or they can get you down. Every game is a renewed opportunity to prove your ability and sometimes to redeem yourself from such a loss. Julie mentions that my confidence had improved, which was true, and this was the most important part of the whole article. Self-confidence can be difficult to acquire and so easy to lose. It also mentioned the Loughborough Supporters Club and those at Heanor and Belper that I was proud to be involved with, which was all true, and the vital importance of the fans to any club, which is also true of course.

Confidence or not, we lost the next three games; Charlton Athletic 1-0, Carlisle United 4-1, and Birmingham City 3-0 in the League Cup. On 8th October we desperately needed a win from our visitors Barnsley, but we had Brian Attley, John Barton, and Steve Buckley all on the injury list and Paul Hooks was suspended, so it didn't look good. The teams were evenly matched at the start with neither side making many attempts at goal until I took a blow on the leg from Stuart Gray which needed some brief attention from our super sponge man Gordon Guthrie. Jake Findlay, my opposite, then made a couple of quality saves from Kevin Wilson and Steve Powell earning us some corners which were cleared with no problem to Barnsley. We were now attacking well with the ball in their half most of the time but we still went into the break at 0-0. We were quietly confident we could at least hold them to a draw at this point, but ideally we were looking for goals.

The second half was busy at their end again with John Robertson and Bobby Davison keeping Jake Findlay occupied for a while until the 65th minute when it all came my way as Tony Cunningham belted one past me after a well-timed pass from Stuart Gray. It must have been a good goal because I never even got a touch to it! I then blocked two more shots from Ronnie Glavin and Billy Ronson as the danger seemed to stay in our half. It was Ronnie Glavin's persistence that gave Barnsley their second, only three minutes from the end when he took advantage of a weak clearance from Dave Watson, ending the game 2-0. My leg was still really painful and so I limped off to some warm applause from a few Derby fans, despite the loss.

After our rare but very welcome 1-0 win at Crystal Palace on 15th October thanks to a goal from John Robertson we had three successive losses. Huddersfield Town kept me very busy on 22nd October when I had to make several challenging saves to stop Brian Stanton and Colin Russell and a full diving save to stop a header from Mark Lillis. They kept up the pressure, hitting several shots wide until I saved a powerful ball from Dave Cowling that was destined for the back of my net, followed by a Brian Stanton shot that flew safely over the bar. I punched a Phil Wilson shot over the bar too before a perfectly placed Colin Russell cross found Mark Lillis who headed in past me just before half-time. The way they were persistently getting through and taking these shots at my goal it was almost inevitable they'd eventually succeed, and I have to say again, where was my defence?

The second half was no different as I stopped one from Brian Stanton in the first few minutes. We made a counter-attack which sadly didn't amount to anything, and Huddersfield came back hard with Colin Russell beating me with a well-timed header in the 62nd minute. Huddersfield must have thought this was their way to beat me because in the 82nd minute Dave Cowling headed one into my net, ending the game 3-0.

I was disappointed in the score line of course, but this was another of those curious games in which we lost but my own performance was widely praised, even though I'd let in three goals, maybe because it could so easily have ended 10-0, not 3-0. We then lost to Birmingham City 4-0 in the League Cup (7-0 on aggregate) and Grimsby Town 2-1. The slide continued. Football managers are right after all: it's all about getting the goals.

We won just four of the remaining ten games of 1983, and sadly 1984 started in a similar fashion, winning just four of the first eleven games. On 10th March 1984 we travelled to Home Park in Devon for a game against Plymouth Argyle in the 6th round of the FA Cup. Despite being in the Third Division Plymouth were enjoying good form and put us under a huge amount of pressure right from the start. But we'd brought some brilliant support with us in the form of 8,500 fans, which was amazing considering the distance.

I was in action against Gordon Staniforth within a few minutes and then Gordon Nisbet after a corner. Paul Hooks blasted one straight at my opposite, Geoff Crudgington, which he handled really well to keep out before an Andy Rogers shot from twenty yards did the same to me. There was yet another attempt from Gordon Staniforth that I managed to deflect as Plymouth never seemed to give up. It was 0-0 at half-time and when we resumed play Plymouth came back at us again, almost straight away. I was forced to make a diving save to stop Gordon Staniforth again, and quickly blocked another from Andy Rogers. To be fair, Kenny Burns, on loan to us from Leeds, did well in defence against an incredibly determined opposition. At the final whistle I was very pleased I'd managed to keep a clean sheet under the circumstances as it ended 0-0 for a replay at home, which we had only four days later.

We quickly realised Plymouth were still determined and this time it didn't end so well. We gifted a goal to them in the 18th minute when Andy Rogers scored directly from the corner post; yes, I know, it was my fault. How many times does a corner kick lead directly to a goal like that? I wrongly assumed it was going well over the top but as it passed over my head I realised to my horror that it was heading into the net, where it indeed landed. In mitigation John Barton was standing inside our goal amongst the netting at the back, for some reason, and could have helped stop it, but he didn't. What he was doing there I've no idea. You can see it on *YouTube*. I think he was crabbing at the time, and that's not a football expression, it's a saying used by fishermen. Typically in football and more so in goalkeeping, I'd been the hero of the previous game but now I was lower than the village idiot. I felt massive disappointment for both myself and the fans. There were more problems when Lindsay Smith hit the bar and Paul Futcher kept a Kevin Hodges header off the line, followed by Smith hitting the post. We were lucky to keep the final score at only 1-0.

If there was one good thing that came from our visit to Plymouth Argyle, it was seeing the fabulous Devon countryside. This had a greater impact on me than I realised at the time, just when Julie and I were considering having a family. There was more to life than Derby County, and even though I had an immense loyalty to the club and the fans, seeing a potential life at other clubs began to interest me.

In April 1984 Peter Taylor retired again, this time for good. It was sad to see him go, but we were in serious trouble at the bottom of division two and there were no signs of improvement. Arthur Cox took over as manager with Roy McFarland as his deputy.

Derby then offered me a three year contract starting at £275 and rising to £325 a week, for the next three years. To be honest I thought this was an insult, particularly when I knew for a fact that a much older member of the team was already paid £800 a week. Money wasn't the primary motivating factor before, but the prospect of becoming a family man with all the associated responsibilities changed my opinion, as it does most people. Not only this, I considered myself a reasonable goalkeeper, so why was there such a pay discrepancy within the team? Clubs often relied on local players wanting to stay local and so there was clearly the temptation to pay them less, which I can understand. A move to another club far away could cause major upheaval to a family, particularly if children are involved with changes of schools and so on. But this was the start of a very competitive era for footballers' salaries, which some say has recently got out of control. I'd heard Yakka Banovic was given a signing-on fee of £10,000 when he joined us four years before in 1980, something I missed of course, having started as a schoolboy. It was common for players like me who'd been with the same club for years to be given a loyalty bonus, not on the scale of a signing-on fee, but something to keep them happy at the club. With all this in mind I asked for a one-off £5,000 loyalty bonus. It was refused. We all knew the club was in serious financial difficulties so this was a disappointment but not a surprise.

Arthur said to me: 'I've seen you play crap, average, and brilliant. The contract still stands, so if you want it, then sign it, but do it quick.'

I didn't sign, not yet, and kept my eyes open. A few weeks later Tommy Doherty came to watch a game at the Raynesway training ground. It was good to see him again and he looked tanned and very healthy after a few years living in Australia managing Sydney Olympic FC. He was now manager of Wolves and we had a few quiet words. On a pleasantly warm but windy afternoon by the Derby ring road he offered me £450 a week for the first year, but with no signing-on fee. He said he couldn't afford a lump sum payment as Wolves had recently been in liquidation. This was a worry. I might move there or spend a lot of time commuting only to find financial disaster waiting for me. I politely declined Tommy's offer, though I was very tempted. I've often wondered whether I did the right thing turning down Wolves. They were a good club and as you can see now they recovered from their financial problems.

I confided in my best mate at Derby County, Steve Buckley. Steve's wife Vera was now working with Julie at the same estate agent's office in Nottingham, we socialised together frequently, and were pretty close. I knew his brother Alan was managing Walsall FC at the time, and he suggested I speak to him. What had I got to lose? I'd never considered them before but I went ahead and spoke to Alan, who was very positive. I was offered a weekly wage higher than that offered by Derby, but what really drew me in was a fantastic signing-on fee of £17,500. I was still only twenty-three with a mortgage and plans to become a family man. After the briefest of discussions with Julie and mutual nodding of heads, a contract was drawn up which I signed without further hesitation. It was just too good to resist. It's odd to think that if Derby had offered me just £5,000 I might not have looked elsewhere and stayed, at least for a while longer.

16

I played my last game for Derby County on 12th May 1984 against Shrewsbury Town. We lost 3-0 to a crowd of less than 6,000. The loss didn't mean I'd given up on them, far from it. It would have been nice to have ended with a win or at least a clean sheet. My professionalism continued until the very end and I tried my best even in the last game. I wasn't the only member of the team to play a final game for Derby County; it was the last one for Dave Watson and Archie Gemmill too.

Walsall was too far to commute so Julie and I put our Nottingham house up for sale. It was sold pretty quickly and in the summer of 1984 we moved to a fantastic three-bedroom detached house in the lovely village of Barton-under-Needwood in Staffordshire, a mile from the A38 between Burton-upon-Trent and Lichfield, ideally located for Walsall. By strange coincidence Arthur Cox, Derby's manager, was living in the same village. Once we'd settled in I'd often pass his house on my four-mile runs but I'd never actually see him. Many years later I visited Arthur and as I approached his house he was mowing his front lawn. His first words were 'Bloody hell!' We shook hands and I asked him how he was, and he reciprocated. He was warm and friendly, and I don't know why I thought he'd be anything other than this. Perhaps it was the way I left Derby County I felt I still didn't have proper closure from the ending of such an important part of my life. I told him I regretted leaving the club when I did, and that I should have stayed longer. He said to me: 'No problem. You went on to better things, I've followed your progress and you've had a great career, Steve.' We only spoke for a few minutes but I felt much better for it.

I was made very welcome at Fellows Park, The Saddlers' home ground at the time. Alan Buckley and his assistant Gary Pendrey were full of enthusiasm for my arrival, and it was infectious. Any lingering doubts I may have had about playing for a Third Division team quickly evaporated. If I'd stayed at Derby County I'd have been playing in the Third Division anyway, as just after my departure they were relegated again. It was only the second time since they were established in 1884 they found themselves in the Third Division. I gained a new car too, a sponsored vehicle from the local Nissan dealer in Wolverhampton. It would be 'Steve Cherry drives a Nissan Cherry' from then on, written in colourful letters down each side.

My first game for Walsall was on 25th August 1984 against York City. We started well when Richard O'Kelly scored quickly from a Peter Hart free kick, beating my opposite Roger Jones. I've no doubt they will have had a typical half-time losers input from their manager and ex-player Denis Smith, because when play resumed they came at us in very determined fashion. Gary Ford and Keith Walwyn came charging through our defence and a hard shot from Keith passed by me straight into my net. John Byrne then had a go but I blocked his shot quite easily, mainly because it came straight at me! Ian Handysides made a cracking shot at the York goal which flew only a few inches over the bar and a shot from Richard O'Kelly was cleared off their goal line by Chris Evans. Both teams played well and created a lot of chances and so the final result of 1-1 was fair. I really enjoyed the game but couldn't help noticing the smaller crowd, at just over 4,000. Did this matter? I was being paid the same, if a little more, and the football was more enjoyable because it seemed far less pressured. I didn't feel playing for Walsall was a retrograde step for my career in any way; I was too busy enjoying playing football and life in Barton-under-Needwood was fantastic.

In our next game, against Swansea City in the League Cup, I had a great time as I kept a clean sheet, winning 2-0. Then at Brentford on 1st September we lost 1-0. This was one of those games I enjoyed despite losing, another occasion when I made several saves I was proud of and came in for some decent compliments as a result. It's easier to lose if it's clear you tried really hard and things could have been much worse. We played Swansea City again on 4th September in the League Cup and thrashed them 3-1, which was 5-1 on aggregate. We then had two draws, a win and two losses, but thankfully the losses were noticeably fewer in number than at Derby County.

I had a good game against Bristol City on 29th September. Dave Kelly got our first goal in three minutes to which Bristol didn't equalise until the second half, and then Richard O'Kelly scored two more for us in quick succession, in the 61st and 65th minutes. While Bristol were still licking their wounds Dave Bamber got our fourth from fifteen yards, beating my opposite John Shaw in the 73rd minute. The fact the game ended 4-1 to us wasn't the reason it was a great game to me; it was because they made some very determined efforts to score, particularly in the last ten minutes. Time after time I had to keep them out and I was very pleased with my performance. A good game with a win attached had been a rarity for me for quite some time, and so this was very welcome!

There was definitely a very different atmosphere at Walsall, which I noticed straight away. It was a great family club, much more so than Derby County at that time, with many more families attending games making it seem generally more amicable. I made some good friendships such as with midfield player Steve Daley, and I quickly developed a great rapport with the Walsall fans, both on the pitch and in the club lounge. Steve and I realised we had the same sense of humour and taste for beer and became great mates. Not everyone was pleased to see me though, as is bound to happen wherever you go in life; I'd replaced Ron Green as first choice goalkeeper and Ron's mate and central defender Colin Brazier took an immediate dislike to me as a result. After one game in which we lost he shouted loudly to me across a packed dressing room 'We should have had Ron in goal.' On 23rd October 1984 we played Derby County in the first occasion I'd confronted my old club. I was getting a lot of stick from the Derby fans, which is always the case when you leave a club, it's an occupational hazard. Brazier knew this of course and so decided to have some fun at my expense. Above all the usual noise of the game he shouted in my direction loud enough for the Derby fans to hear 'You fucking wanker!' They loved it.

We won five of our next six games and on 24th November I was back in Devon playing Plymouth Argyle. They were struggling at the time but were first to score in the 47th minute when Tommy Tynan got a low shot past me. This seemed to shake us into action as Ian Handysides, Craig Shakespeare and Gary Childs each scored past my opposite Geoff Crudgington. In a repeat of the Bristol City game I was then very busy as they kept on attacking relentlessly, but I successfully denied them more goals, leaving us with our fourth successive away win at 3-1.

I was thoroughly enjoying myself at Walsall; I was playing well and getting favourable reports as a result, and I was getting noticed. On 15th December we were at a very cold and foggy Boothferry Park for a game against Hull City. I could hardly see the ball so I was chuffed to keep a clean sheet until the 47th minute when I was beaten by a powerful header from Billy Whitehurst following a low corner from Billy Askew. I was particularly annoyed because I'd kept them out with some great saves up until then, and only a few minutes before with a full stretch fingertip save knocking the ball onto the crossbar. Even though we'd lost I'd played to the best of my ability, and again, it was one of those games that could have ended much worse. Eric Greenwood in *The Sunday People* said I'd made seven top class saves (I wasn't counting!), with two of them being 'quite unbelievable.' He said my performance had been 'superb.' Thanks Eric.

Our last game of the year was against Lincoln City on 29th December and it ended 0-0. Each side made plenty of chances but my opposite Dave Felgate and I made sure we kept it goalless so that we'd both get our clean sheet bonus!

1985 began poorly for Walsall with a loss of 4-1 to Doncaster Rovers on New Year's Day and then a few days later we faced York City in the FA Cup. This was going to be a memorable day for me, but not because of the football; Julie went into labour at one o'clock on the Friday night/Saturday morning before the game at Bootham Crescent. Obviously I was with her, and was still with her at the hospital at five o'clock in the morning when she was still in labour. I'd been told I couldn't miss the game so we decided I had to go home and get a couple of hours' sleep. I returned at eight o'clock but she was still in labour! At nine o'clock I was picked up from outside the Little Chef on the A38 by the Walsall team bus for the hundred mile journey up to York. I was absolutely shattered and slept most of the way.

We lost 3-0, which was hardly surprising really, but I did try my best, honest! Jonathan was born just after the game ended while I was in the dressing rooms at Bootham Crescent. Julie's mum Joan was present during the birth and I finally saw him for the first time just before eight o'clock that night. Later on I celebrated in The Three Crowns pub in Barton.

On 26th January we faced Millwall. A cold snap had just ended and the Molineux ground had thawed quickly with heavy rain causing it to become more than a little boggy. It was like being back at the Baseball Ground. This never happened at Fellows Park, which had one of the best pitches I've ever played on. The ground itself wasn't brilliant, but Walsall's turf was always in great condition, thanks to groundskeeper Roger who was so good at his job he later looked after the hallowed ground of Wembley Stadium.

There were three pitch inspections before we began; the Molineux turf was so bad that day. Once underway I blocked a couple of early shots from Steve Lowndes and Nicky Chatterton but it was otherwise uneventful. So much so that when it ended 0-0 the fans from both sides expressed their disapproval with a few of them booing us as we walked off. I suppose they were right to complain; it was our job to provide entertainment they'd paid for, and so if we don't deliver the goods then we are no different to other performers such as actors, musicians and singers. But it is never a pleasant experience, and thankfully quite rare. I was glad to keep a clean sheet; for a goalkeeper this is not just a matter of personal pride, it often meant a cash reward too, the 'clean sheet bonus' as it's called, though some clubs don't do it. It's usually not a fortune, just a few hundred quid, more as a reward than an incentive, but now I was a family man, every penny helped.

We had a chance to redeem ourselves with our fans a week later against Bristol City. My opposite Ian Leigh made a dreadful mistake early on when he mishandled a back pass allowing Dave Kelly to knock it into the net. Such long back-passes are unnecessary, often risky, and unpopular with fans, and I don't encourage them. They can slow down the pace of a game and as such they are often used for deliberate time-wasting. Craig Shakespeare then got our second after a free kick. This game was full of fouls and free kicks; three of our players were booked including assistant manager Gary Pendrey when he ran onto the pitch to treat an injured Gary Childs, and City's Howard Pritchard was sent off for kicking Phil Hawker. Bobby Hutchinson got one past me despite my diving attempt at a save when Richard O'Kelly mistakenly passed to Alan Walsh, ending the game 2-1.

On 6th February 1985 we played Derby County again, this time in the Freight Rover Trophy. I was subjected to a tirade of chanting and abuse from the Derby fans for the entire ninety minutes, virtually non-stop. It's an occupational hazard, as I said, but it still gets to you, particularly if they shout things about your family, which is unfair. You can't run down the field to get away from it either; you're stuck there, stranded between the sticks. On this occasion they were singing, 'She's here, she's there, she's every fucking where, Cherry's wife, Cherry's wife!' When I told Julie about this she was understandably upset and we decided she would never attend another Derby game. On this occasion we lost 1-0. Maybe they put me off. I'd never admit that of course, if you do it means they've won. I'm just glad hardly anyone saw it, as the gate was less than 4,000.

Revenge is sweet though; two weeks later we played Derby again in the Freight Rover Trophy and we thrashed them 5-3. It really was a case of 'you're not laughing anymore.' Some of their fans even left before the end. I bumped into Fred Fern, one of the directors of Derby County after the game, and he said to me in hushed tones 'Walsall beat Derby because of the goalkeeper. No comparison.' This was flattering for me, but not much of an endorsement of their current goalkeeper, Eric Steele.

We then had three more wins on the trot, to Leyton Orient, 4-2, York City, 3-0 (nice to get that score reversed!) and Newport County, 2-1. On 6th March we lost 2-0 in a League game, to Derby County, of all people, and that hurt. It's funny how you forget the bad times and the bad games! I can't remember much about this game, but that's not surprising is it? I was subjected to the same abuse again for the entire ninety minutes, I do remember that.

I needed a lift and I got one only three days later in a game against Swansea City. My opposite, Mike Hughes, was beaten early on when Richard O'Kelly scored from a rebound and then Steve Elliott scored from a free kick. I deflected some very determined shots from Steve Mardenborough and Ray McHale, but Swansea's fate was sealed when Steve Elliott headed in his second and our third after a free kick. I was then kept busy by Colin Pascoe and Dean Saunders but successfully kept them out, the game staying at 3-0 until the end, winning another clean sheet bonus.

The rest of the season was mixed; we had six wins, nine losses, and four draws. Not brilliant. But at the end of the season I was truly humbled when the Walsall fans voted me their Player of the Year. What a fantastic compliment. I really was genuinely chuffed to bits.

17

I had settled in well at Fellows Park and the new 1985/86 season began better than the end of the previous one, with seven wins, one draw, and only two losses until the Leeds game on 25th September. I was kept very busy in the first half and then watched on as my opposite Mervyn Day was in action working hard against Steve Elliott and Gary Childs, until between us we kept the final score at 0-0, another clean sheet. A win against Newport County, 2-0, then losses against Wigan Athletic, 2-0, and Doncaster Rovers, 1-0, saw us playing Leeds United again on 7th October, this time in the League Cup. We lost 3-0.

Then after a 2-2 draw against Plymouth Argyle we played Wolves on 19th October at Molineux again, hoping for a win. I stopped a great shot from Derek Ryan that I was very proud of, and my opposite Scott Barrett, standing in for an injured Tim Flowers, also worked hard, ending the game 0-0. After losing 2-1 to Brentford we won 3-0 at Darlington before we had another goalless draw on 2nd November when we played Notts County; I'd like to say I saved a penalty by using calculated goalkeeping skill, but Mark Goodwin's spot kick hit my right hand post and not me!

To say we had mixed fortunes after this is a huge understatement, because we then beat Cardiff City 6-3, but immediately after that lost to Gillingham 5-2. How does that happen? Such is football.

On 16th November we played Preston North End in another extraordinary goal-filled game in the FA Cup. Willie Naughton and Steve Elliott scored early on sending us 2-0 up. I then kept out a great shot from Vernon Alliatt, followed quickly by our third goal from Gary Childs. Willie Naughton then got his second before John Thomas got Preston's first past me, with all this happening in a very breathless opening twenty-five minutes. After half-time Gary Childs,

Richard O'Kelly and Willie Naughton each beat my opposite Phil Harrington, bringing our tally up to seven. I couldn't believe it. Gary Brazil and Mick Martin each got one past me despite my best efforts, with the game finally ending at 7-3. It was a shame this extraordinary game wasn't witnessed by more than the 3,000 who were there on the day. I was happy but totally exhausted and it was another game that reminded me of those happy days on Calverton Pit Field. My dad would have said 'They got their two bob's worth that day.'

The following week we did well to hold Blackpool to a 1-1 draw; Steve Hetzke, Colin Greenall, and Nicky Law each tried very hard to beat me again after Colin Greenall's goal. I certainly didn't need to do many stretching exercises for a few days afterwards as I had plenty of practice during that game! We then lost 2-1 to Bury before two FA Cup games, holding Port Vale to a 0-0 draw and then beating them 2-1 in the replay. We then continued our winning streak with 4-2 at AFC Bournemouth, 2-1 at Lincoln City and 3-1 at home to York City. We were on a roll.

When we were due to play Manchester City in the FA Cup on 4th January 1986 we were hopeful of at least a draw; we were enjoying good form, our confidence was high, and Man City were not playing brilliantly at the time. But we hadn't taken account of the weather, which was appalling, to say the least. It should probably never have taken place but the referee Dennis Hedges allowed it to begin and to continue. It was bitterly cold at Maine Road, the pitch was rock solid, and heavy snow was drifting in from the Pennines. It was proper snow too, in huge flakes, you know the sort, almost the size of your hand, flying through the air like Frisbees before settling quickly on already frozen ground.

We started really well, before the worst of the snow, when Richard O'Kelly almost scored past my opposite Eric Nixon; a cross from Willie Naughton gave him a great shot at goal, saved only by Eric's frozen legs, which even from a hundred yards away I could see had a distinctly blue tinge to them. It could have been his tracksuit bottoms of course. Steve Daley then took a shot on the rebound which flew straight over the bar, much to the relief and amusement of the City fans. They whooped and cheered particularly loudly because Steve was an ex-City player, and an expensive one at that, at £1.4m six years before. They shouted 'What a waste of money!' almost every time he touched the ball. City then gifted us a great opportunity; Mick McCarthy brought down Richard O'Kelly in the Man City penalty area. Mick shouldn't even have been there that day, because he replaced Steve Elliott who was injured. Mick decided to take the spot kick himself in what was now a whirling snowstorm, and easily beat

Eric Nixon sending us 1-0 up. To be fair to him Eric probably couldn't even see the ball, white against a white background, but for us this was a brilliant start.

Man City came back at us immediately when Paul Power hit the bar above my head as the snow continued to worsen; the pitch markings almost disappeared, visibility dropped to just a few yards and players were sliding around as though on ice skates. I saved shots from Mark Lillis and Gordon Davies but City just kept on coming as the ball was tossed around like a giant snowball. Every time I made a save I felt like I was landing on concrete, it was so bloody painful. Paul Simpson took a corner which found Gordon Davies who then got their equaliser with a crafty backward header straight past me and into the net, just before half-time. Even in my gloves my finger ends were numb with cold.

During the break there were some heated discussions between the linesmen and the referee about the pitch and the dreadful weather conditions. Many of us doubted it would continue, as we all stood around cradling cups of hot sweet tea, the energy drink of the day, but the snow was apparently easing and so the call came into the dressing room after fifteen minutes for play to resume.

It's not often a goalkeeper can blame the weather, but on this occasion I feel justified. Not long into the second half disaster struck when Peter Hart's back pass to me was held up in the snow to such an extent the ball rolled to a near dead stop far too early and more than ten yards away from me. What did I say about long back-passes? Paul Simpson was there like a vulture waiting to pounce and seized the opportunity to flick the ball straight past me, completely out of my reach and into the net. Peter realised his mistake straight away. I just hoped he and everyone else in our team would learn from it and not repeat it.

From then on City just seemed to be all over us, only confirming their higher status. Apart from one more attempt at their goal by Richard O'Kelly I was kept warm and busy by City players almost constantly in our half. As so often happens their last one came only a minute from the end when Paul Simpson blasted a shot from only ten yards out which I didn't get a touch to, ending the game 3-1. As cold as it was, and it was one of the coldest I've ever played in, I thoroughly enjoyed the game and made some good saves, even though every time I did it seemed like I landed on solid rock. It was great to play Man City, and such opportunities are fantastic for the smaller clubs, I never tired of them and it reinforced my continued love and appreciation for the FA Cup.

We then lost two, won one, and drew one before we thrashed Third Division leaders Reading 6-0 in a fantastic game on 1st February. We were on form, they were not. I was thrilled to keep a clean sheet but felt sorry for my opposite Gary Westwood, as I knew exactly how he felt. We won the Fiat 'Team of the Week' award that day and £500 which we donated to a local boys' club.

On 5th February we played Brentford. Like us, they had their sights on promotion and so for us a win would be extremely useful, but they were the only team to have beaten us at home that season, back in October when we lost 2-1. The game started badly when Rowan Alexander beat me from six yards out, a low ball that passed to my right. They were playing well, as Andy Sinton and Tony Lynch dominated the midfield, keeping us out for a while as Terry Hurlock then took a shot which I had to dive full stretch to keep out, followed by another shot from Tony Lynch.

We then had our half-time loser's team talk from manager Alan Buckley. Our defence was clearly lacking, we desperately needed a goal, and so we had to just get stuck in; the usual advice. Steve knew if the pressure was kept up on me they'd eventually get one past me. It must have worked, as immediately after the whistle we went on the attack; Nick Cross beat my opposite Gary Philips, followed quickly by Peter Hart, and then Craig Shakespeare: Three goals in six minutes; I couldn't believe it. There isn't a football manager on earth that wouldn't want to bottle that kind of sudden turnaround and motivation. If only. Drop for drop it would be worth more than the very best Champagne.

The rest of the season was pretty good for Walsall, with seven wins, five draws, and only six losses. The losses weren't disastrous and we finished in May 1986 sixth place in the League, just below Gillingham and above York City. Reading, Plymouth Argyle, and Derby County all went up. Even though I was no longer a Derby County player it was good to see them go back up into the Second Division and playing well.

Inexplicably for some in charge at Walsall our performance wasn't good enough though, and on 1st June Alan Buckley and Gary Pendrey were sacked. I was shocked. It certainly is a fickle business. I'd lost the two men who had put their faith in me and had taken me on, men who had become friends as well as managers.

The club had been bought by millionaire Terry Ramsden who immediately appointed Tommy Coakley, a former Scottish player and now a coach, as manager. After the initial surprise none of this would have mattered to me. I was having a great time at Walsall, it was a good club and the fans were terrific. But Tommy brought his own goalkeeper, Mark Prudhoe, who was now going to be first choice. I knew Mark, he was a nice chap. It wasn't his fault I was suddenly demoted to the Reserves, but it hurt nonetheless. Other players were bought and sold and so you could say I was lucky to still be there. But playing in the Reserves was not what I wanted to do, so reluctantly I began to look around, and was granted permission to approach other clubs.

I therefore began the 1986/87 season playing in the Walsall FC Reserve team. As though fate hadn't treated me badly enough I then injured my right thumb while training, in a point-blank save. It wasn't broken but it may as well have been; it was very badly sprained and swelled up to look like something very odd from *Star Trek*. So now I wasn't even in the Reserves, but sitting on the bench, watching.

I still wanted to feel part of it all and so I attended training sessions and on one occasion travelled with the Walsall Youth Team to the Raynesway in Derby, to watch a match against their Youth Team. It was great to see the old place again and to my astonishment I was asked to sit on the subs' bench, despite my pointing out I wasn't actually there to play, but to watch.

At half-time Derby were leading 1-0 and were delighted that they'd progress further in the Midland Intermediate League if they won. I saw Arthur Cox and Ray McFarland shouting encouragement to their lads, and I knew they'd seen me but they didn't make any effort to speak. Further disaster struck Walsall when one of our midfield players became injured and had to come off. We had no-one to replace him, until they turned to me.

My right arm was in a sling, my thumb was bandaged up, and I had no kit with me. What could I do? What would anyone do? I took off the sling and put on some spare kit. I borrowed a pair of size ten boots which were far too big (I'm size eight), which looked and felt like an old pair of skis. I ran onto the pitch to 'Chez, play up front, just do what you can, okay?' So I did what I could. It seemed very odd to be playing in the outfield and I wish I'd had a camera to capture the moment when Arthur and Ray saw me running with the ball against their team.

I didn't really expect to make an impact on the game, let alone score a goal, but ten minutes from the end as a high ball came over for their goalkeeper Mark Grew I stuck my head in the way and knocked the ball into their net. He couldn't believe it, and frankly neither could I. There were wild shouts of approval and lots of leaping about from the Walsall bench at this unexpected equaliser. From the Derby bench there was absolute silence with huge rolls of tumbleweed drifting by until I heard Arthur Cox shout: 'How the fuck can you let him score?!' It was truly hilarious, and I couldn't stop laughing. The local press had a great time with headlines such as 'Cherry Ripe!' in *The Green 'Un* and 'Cherry scores late equalizer!' It was a lot of fun.

It was around this time I rang Dave Smith at Plymouth Argyle. He was surprised to hear from me, but pleased at the same time. I spoke to Tommy about it and he wasn't surprised, but he also said I was free to speak to whoever I wanted. I then told him Dave had agreed to me attending Home Park for a week's trial with Plymouth Argyle.

Dad and Mum, Harold Hector and Lenorah Cherry, in the 1950s.

William Lee Junior School Under 11s, celebrating
winning the Nottinghamshire Schools Treble, 1970.

Left to right: Clive Whiting, me, Kevin Ray (kneeling), Rob Watts, Terry
Davidson, Tommy Robinson, Ian Huthwaite, Richard Tomlinson, Bruce
Drysdale, Paul Lewis (kneeling), Ricky Morley, Paul Naisbitt, Anthony
Perkins. Adults, left to right: Mr Jackson (Head teacher), ex-Notts County
footballer Tommy Lawton, and Mr Chapman (teacher and coach).

In training kit at The Raynesway, Derby, early 1980s.

One of my best performances: Sat 19th Feb 1983, The Baseball Ground, Derby County v Manchester United, FA Cup 5th Round, 1-0 to Manchester United. Left to right: Gordon McQueen, Steve Powell, George Foster, Steve Coppell, Remi Moses, Andy Hill and Mick Brolly.

With manager Neil Warnock, standing on the Meadow Lane pitch, on my first
day at Notts County, 16th February 1989.

Publicity shot at Notts County,
with my sponsored Sondico gloves prominent!

With some of the team celebrating at Wembley, Sunday 27th May 1990, as
Notts County win the Third Division Play-off Final. Left to right: Mark Draper,
Charlie Palmer, Kevin Bartlett, Phil Turner, Craig Short (obscured), me,
Gary Chapman holding the trophy.

Notts County's official club photo of the great occasion.

NOTTS COUNTY FOOTBALL CLUB
3rd Division Play-off Winners

WEMBLEY STADIUM
Sunday 27th May 1990

Notts County Player of the Year, May 1992.

Notts County v Nottingham Forest, Meadow Lane 12th Feb 1994,
'Charlie Palmer Day.'

Remonstrating to the defence during the same game, with Andy Legg in the
background and Forest's Lee Glover probably getting an earful!

My family on my wedding day to Fiona, 11th October 2013. Left to right: Elouise with Oliver, Fiona, me, Chloe, Jonathan with Joshua, and Emma.

With Fiona on our wedding day, 11th October 2013.

My grandsons Oliver and Joshua, in Notts County strip of course!

The last photo of Mum before she died a few days after this was taken.

A proud moment for me: With one of my all-time heroes Sir Gordon Banks at
a goalkeepers' reunion dinner, Chesterfield FC, August 2018.

At Chesterfield FC, August 2018.

18

On 20th November 1986 I signed with Plymouth Argyle for £19,000, with a signing-on fee of £18,000. Plymouth seemed a lovely place to live and bring up children: Julie was pregnant again and so we were both looking to the future. I really enjoyed my time at Walsall and I've since heard I was their fourth top goalkeeper in fifty years, which is a great accolade. It was nice to leave on good terms, but I didn't want to play in Reserves, and I was excited about starting a new life with my family on the south coast. In the meantime we kept our house in Barton, where Julie and Jonathan would stay until I was fully settled. I lived at the Santa Barbara guest house in Plymouth, run by a lovely Irish couple, Noel and Mary, and I'd drive home as often as I could. Julie would bring Jonathan down for visits and when the guest house was closed over Christmas we stayed at the Mayflower Hotel for a few days, all paid for by the club. I also lived in the Continental Hotel for a while, still commuting home whenever I could.

Plymouth Argyle's goalkeeper Geoff Crudgington, or 'Crudge' as he was affectionately known, had been at Home Park for seven years, was approaching his mid-thirties, and was very popular both in the team and with the fans, as I was soon to find out. The coach, Stewart Houston still hadn't made up his mind as to when I would make my debut, but he must have known there may have been some adverse reactions from the fans. I sat on the bench to watch the Oldham Athletic game 29th November in which Geoff put in a good performance with Plymouth winning 3-2, but it could be argued that the two goals Geoff conceded should have been kept out. The local press certainly thought so, and were now asking when I would be given my chance. Manager Dave Smith understood this and said 'We didn't bring Steve Cherry here to play in the reserves. Geoff's been in the game long enough to know the score.'

We hadn't lost for the last five games, so Geoff would be a hard act to follow, but I was more than ready. My call up came on 6th December against Stoke City at the Victoria Ground. I worked hard and was having a good game keeping out several determined chances from Nicky Morgan and Carl Saunders until disaster in the 64th minute. Clive Goodyear was penalised for pushing Carl Saunders and George Berry then blasted a kick from the spot which beat me despite applying my usual psychology. Suddenly I was the bogey man in the eyes of the Plymouth fans, even after stopping Tony Kelly and Carl Saunders in full stretch diving saves. My opposite, Peter Fox, a veteran in his 250th League appearance, did well to stop Tommy Tynan, and I stopped a drive from Brian Talbot in a move that a circus acrobat would have been proud of, to keep the final score at 1-0. Fred Yates in *The News of The World* later said I'd made 'a polished performance' in my debut and he named me Man of the Match. But it wasn't enough for the Plymouth Argyle fans, many of whom were openly hostile.

Our next game on 13th December was against Derby County, in my home debut at Plymouth. It couldn't have been a worse prospect; I knew I'd face hostility from the Derby fans and now I was getting the same from some of our own. Manager Dave Smith collected the coveted Manager of the Month award before the game and as soon as it began I was busy. We were just above Derby in the table who were doing well again at third from the top of Division Two, but with the same number of points, so they really wanted to beat us, and it showed. They kept on attacking and dominating play until the 37th minute when Gary Micklewhite beat me with a great shot I had no chance stopping. After the break we faced much the same. I made a series of tough saves from Bobby Davison and Gary Micklewhite which Dave Wharton in *The Sunday People* later said were 'incredible examples of razor sharp reflexes,' giving me eight out of ten for my performance. I don't know about that, I was just trying my best, aware that I had to prove myself to my home fans, and not give my old team an easy ride. Their striker Phil Gee took several shots that on each occasion had me at full stretch to keep safe. We tried our best in reply as Kevin Hodges hit the bar above the head of my opposite Mark Wallington and as the game reached ninety minutes it seemed we would resign ourselves to a loss, and my second in a row. Then twenty seconds into injury time Kevin Hodges was fouled by Mick Forsyth and John Matthews launched the ball into a congested Derby penalty area where Tommy Tynan headed into their net. Seconds later the referee blew the full-time whistle, ending it at 1-1. The Derby fans were choked, while I was very relieved.

Sadly for me we lost most of the next dozen games and the fans were letting me know how they felt about it. Before the game with Arsenal on 31st January they booed and shouted abuse such as 'Get off!' and worse. They must have known what was coming; in the next ninety minutes I was to let in six goals, with Arsenal winning 6-1 in a crushing defeat. I had the same treatment two weeks later when we played Blackburn Rovers. The game began well enough with the Plymouth fans cheering – perhaps sarcastically – every time I made a decent stop and Kevin Summerfield scored past my opposite Terry Genoe with a great header sending us 1-0 up in the first half. But then in the 68th minute Blackburn were awarded a penalty when Gerry McElhinney brought down Glen Keeley. I heard Gerry arguing with the referee about it and so he was also given a booking for his trouble. I applied my usual psychology for the spot kick, but Simon Barker clearly wasn't fooled, and I dived the wrong way. However, lady luck was on my side because the ball struck my right boot and didn't go in. I know it was a fluke, but I stopped it. It still wasn't good enough for the fans.

Tommy Tynan, Garry Nelson and Darren Rowbotham then tried very hard to get our second but my opposite, Bobby Mimms, did well to keep them out. It looked like I'd have my first win at Plymouth until the 87th minute when a free kick was awarded to Blackburn just outside my area. Alan Ainscow took the kick and it sailed right past me into the net, just out of my reach, ending the game 1-1. The Plymouth fans were not shy in letting me know what they thought about it.

In the midst of all this my private life was about to get so much better; on March 1st my gorgeous daughter Emma was born in Burton hospital. This time I was there and not splashing around with a dozen naked men in a huge bath in York.

When I thought my professional life couldn't get any worse, it did. It's a curious thing but when you start to lose your confidence it becomes increasingly difficult to retrieve, and a spiral descent begins which you cannot control. On 14th March we were away at Sunderland and doing well up to half-time at 1-1. I'd made a good save from Dave Buchanan in the 43rd minute to keep the score level. Then in the second half I misread a close ball from Paul Lemon and as I tried to palm it away it flew back into the net. It was obviously my mistake and a costly one I just didn't need. The game ended at 2-1 and this loss was a severe blow to our promotion hopes, for which I took most of the blame.

I needed a good performance, with a win. It came a week later when we hosted Grimsby Town and we thrashed them 5-0. It was a very welcome clean sheet for me, but to be honest it wasn't that difficult, though I was still very relieved. It didn't last. Only a week later we were ourselves thrashed by Leeds United 4-0. You are only as good as your last game, and the fans were back letting me know what they thought of me. I desperately needed some consistently good playing to silence the criticism.

It finally came in the next six games without a loss; the first two being an uneventful 3-2 win against Shrewsbury Town in pouring rain and on a boggy pitch, and a 1-1 draw against Brighton & Hove Albion. I was back on form for our game against Crystal Palace on 11th April. I kept out their very determined strikers Mark Bright and Ian Wright despite their best efforts. My opposite George Wood made some great saves too though, keeping out Tommy Tynan on several occasions. Tommy had been playing well all season and in May was voted Plymouth's Player of the Year. But my best saves came from attempts by Ken O'Doherty and Jim Cannon, whose header I managed to knock over the bar with a full stretch jump, just getting my fingertips to the ball. It was 0-0 at the end, and I'd had a really good game.

Our last game of the season was at the Baseball Ground on 9th May 1987. My old friends Derby County were on the verge of becoming Second Division Champions and gaining promotion, and so a win against us would seal it. We were hoping for a promotion place ourselves via the play-offs, so it was just as important to us. We started brilliantly with a goal from Garry Nelson in only the 9th minute, where it stayed until the break. Their half-time dressing room input from manager Arthur Cox must have involved more than a little flying spittle because they came back at us like a different team. I was forced to make several challenging saves in quick succession until Bobby Davison beat me in the 70th minute with a goal I had no chance stopping, and then Nigel Callaghan put them in the lead in the 81st minute. Two minutes later they got their third past me when Gary Micklewhite scored. In return Garry Nelson then got one back for us past my opposite Mark Wallington saving our blushes a little, but then in the very last minute John Gregory got a fourth past me for Derby, ending it 4-2. The Derby fans clearly loved it, while our own fans were thoroughly unimpressed.

There's no doubt about it, I'd made a poor start to my time at Plymouth Argyle. Manager Dave Smith told me my place in the team was secure, so I was at least reassured by this. But I had my own doubts, however, and was seriously wondering if I'd made a mistake heading to Home Park.

19

I'd lost my form and quite a bit of self-confidence on the pitch. Perhaps I'd been tired and stressed out with all the travelling from Devon up to the Midlands and back? With this in mind in the summer of 1987 we sold up in Barton-under-Needwood and bought a house in Plymouth. It was in Ivy Bridge actually, in Cameron Close, a lovely village big enough to call a small town ten miles outside Plymouth on the A38. It was the first place we looked and after a pub lunch in The Oak, one of the two village pubs, we decided straight away. In addition to the other pub, The Duke of Cornwall, The Sportsman's Club was at the other side of the village and was very popular. Two other Plymouth players also lived there, Nicky Law and Kevin Summerfield.

For a couple of weeks that summer we didn't have our own coach so it was decided we should train with some great local lads who were very highly thought of and knew a thing or two about keeping fit: The Royal Marines. We were waiting for Martin Harvey to arrive from the Far East and take up the role of assistant manager and coach but until then Dave Smith thought it would be a good idea for the whole team to spend two weeks with the Marines. Our team bus took us to their base in Plymouth on the first Monday morning and I'm sure I saw the driver laughing as he drove away. After some brief introductions, with a notable absence of anything resembling health and safety regulations, we began straight away.

We were split into smaller groups and spent time jogging in lines with two Marines at the front and two at the back, the four of them changing places occasionally to keep the pace going. I was doing okay so far and just as I was beginning to think this whole experience would be quite easy each team was then given a telegraph pole. I imagined we'd probably just do some simple lifting exercises with it by picking it up and putting it down but it was far worse than that. Whose mad idea was it, somewhere in the dim and distant past, to try running while carrying what is effectively a massive tree? It was bloody heavy, with straps dotted along its length and seemed to get heavier by the second. You couldn't allow it to bump along on your shoulder because the pain was too great and it would probably break your collar bone. Suddenly it didn't seem quite so easy. One thing's for sure, after stomping around with that damned thing for a while, to be without it was pure heaven.

We were then taken a few miles up the coast to Lympstone and onto their assault course, which I can assure you is much harder than it looks. Climbing up huge nets, scaling walls, and jumping ditches was all quite reasonable but there was an underwater section like a huge concrete pipe ten feet long full of dirty water which the Marines warned us about before entering. 'We have to get here early every morning to clear out the rats and snakes, but there might still be some left in there, so be careful.' It was a filthy dark brown soup with one Marine pushing us down into it at one end while another at the other side dragged us out, with no sight, sound or feeling of anything in between other than total immersion in muddy water. It was summer so it wasn't freezing, but it wasn't heated either. We didn't know for sure whether the story about the rats and snakes was true or not, along with the highest obstacle they warned us about where they said they'd recently lost one of their own when he fell to his death.

Every day we did similar, except at the weekend when we went home and slept for 48 hours solid, too exhausted to do anything else. In the second week we had some light relief when we were taken to a shooting range. We fired all sorts of pistols and rifles and it was great fun. We shot at targets and tin cans against a huge sandbank. They told us one of the rifles was incredibly powerful and had a range of two miles, and so hiding behind a car door like they do in the TV cop programmes was a total waste of time.

Clive Goodyear clearly wasn't listening when we were told how to hold the rifle. Instead of tucking it firmly into his shoulder as instructed he pulled the trigger with it hanging loosely in front of his face; the recoil was tremendous and so the stock flew straight back at him, striking him hard just below the right eye, bursting his skin open. There was blood everywhere. Of course we found this hilarious as he was eventually carried off to hospital in an ambulance. Clive later went on to play for Wimbledon in the FA Cup final against Liverpool, winning 1-0.

After each day's exertion we joined the Marines in the sergeant's mess for a few beers, usually more than just a few actually. They could drink even more beer than footballers, that's for sure.

These were just some of the highlights of our time with the Marines, and I really enjoyed it all. On the last day we took part in a 'yomp' across Dartmoor from Newton Abbot to Princetown, high up on the moors. Until then we'd been wearing our own training kit but now for the grand finale we were issued with regular army gear and boots. Apart from some very expensive well-coiffured footballers' hairstyles most of us could have passed for Marines, at a push, but some looked like civilians thrown into uniforms much like you see in today's reality TV programmes.

The route we should have taken was 21 miles up into Dartmoor across open country, supposedly with five checkpoints along the way. Luckily we were NOT expected to carry a telegraph pole, something which we were very pleased about! We set off in teams of six, three Marines and three players, at ten minute intervals, just before ten o'clock in the morning. At first you could see the team ahead in the distance but then once on the moors all visual contact was lost.

Everything seemed to be going well until five hours in, when it was clear we were still far from civilisation and had not finished as expected. We should have reached the end point by that time, but we missed three checkpoints and were now overdue. The Marines kept repeating the word 'endex' as they argued over which direction to take, true north, or magnetic north, huddled together around a compass while occasionally gazing towards the horizon, and smiling at us. I wasn't worried. It was summer, though the weather up there can change in an instant, luckily it wasn't bad at the time, but I was relieved it wasn't the middle of winter.

The Marines didn't actually tell us we had become 'temporarily unsure of our position,' but we guessed. It became clear when a huge Chinook helicopter appeared from nowhere, thudding overhead, circling around us as if to get a better look as we all waved frantically, the Marines included. The aircrew probably found it all very amusing, gazing down, pointing us in the right direction before thumping away again so low over the hills I thought it might crash. By this time we had to keep stopping to take off our boots, or at least we footballers did. We were all pretty fit, obviously, by comparison to ordinary members of the public, and we earned a great living by wearing boots and standing for ninety minutes, but this was something else. We all had huge blisters the size of which I'd never seen before, and these blisters were made bigger still by other blisters on top of the original blisters. The Marines gave us medication for them called 'Newskin' which we applied liberally before carrying on. I'm wondering now what sort of boots we were given, because I've never seen so many blisters appear so readily. Eventually at six-thirty that night we arrived at Princetown nearly three hours late to a lot of cheering and applause, limping in, exhausted and starving. We then tucked into a barbeque meal set up by the Marines which to this day remains the best I've ever tasted.

It was then, and only then, that we were told the rats, snakes, fatalities, and even getting lost on Dartmoor were all figments of the Marines' imaginations, part of them mightily taking the piss out of us, which of course now only added to the hysterics. Everything else might have been unreal, but the blisters certainly were not!

Back in the real world there's one good thing about descending to your lowest point; there's only one way to go, and that's up. Our first game of the 1987/88 season on 15th August 1987 was against Manchester City. Nicky Law put us in the lead with a great header in the 36th minute, despite us very clearly being the underdogs. Paul Stewart then beat me with a rebound shot I'd kept out from Paul Simpson and near the end Imre Varadi got a lucky shot past me ending the game 2-1. It wasn't too bad considering no-one expected us to win anyway, and I'd played pretty well.

Three days later we unleashed our new record signing, Mark Smith, who came from Sheffield Wednesday at a cost of a whopping £170,000 against Ipswich Town. It made my signing-on fee look like a real bargain. I had all on to stop their new player David Lowe from scoring after he twice tried in quick succession to beat me. Kevin Summerfield, Stewart Evans and Tommy Tynan kept up the pressure on my opposite John Hallworth who played well to keep them out, despite being booked in the 78th minute for time-wasting. Both teams were pleased to see the final score remain at 0-0.

We then beat Huddersfield Town 6-1 and Reading 1-0. I was enjoying myself again, playing well and keeping them all out. On 31st August I was very busy against Sheffield United, but not as busy as my opposite Andy Leaning. He let one in that was ironically from an old team-mate of his, Stewart Evans, in the 37th minute, and that's how it ended at 1-0. Another win. To my surprise and delight I was awarded Man of the Match. Things were looking up at last.

I was really enjoying life in Devon too. On most Sundays we'd find a local beach and even drive the relatively short distance further west into Cornwall. We got to know Alec Rickard who owned The Golden Lion pub in Padstow which is now owned by his son Martin, and we visited Looe quite a lot, just a few miles west of Plymouth. Emma was still a toddler but we had some great times in the area. I was given free membership of the St Mellion golf club in Plymouth and I played there every other Sunday and sometimes on my Wednesday day off (yes, footballers get days off too!).

I played golf with team-mates such as Steve Cooper and Leigh Cooper, and though they shared the same surname, Steve was a Brummie and was definitely not related to Leigh! There were other perks to being a footballer too; Vospers Ford dealers in Plymouth gave me a choice of new cars for a nominal fee of £100 a month. I chose a Scorpio, a big family car, just right for trips north to the Midlands.

As the season progressed we lost 2-1 to Barnsley before we played West Brom on 12th September. This would prove to be a great game, with five goals in the last twenty minutes. I failed to save a penalty and then saved one, with only one of those counting, the one I saved. Leigh Cooper was deemed to have fouled George Reilly, who beat me from the spot. But it was disallowed. This doesn't happen very often! One of their players had moved forward beyond the spot just before the kick. So he took it again, and this time I beat him. On his second spot kick he booted it right where I wanted him to. Andy Gray had scored the first goal of the game against us in the 12th minute and no goals followed until well into the second half. We then scored two goals in five minutes from Tommy Tynan and John Clayton, beating my opposite Stuart Naylor just as our coach Martin Harvey was shouting for John to come off. He obviously didn't want to! George Reilly got one past me before Tommy then got our third followed by Andy Gray equalising in the 85th minute, ending the game 3-3. It certainly frayed the nerves of both sets of fans in some great football entertainment. It's what the game is all about after all, and I really enjoyed it.

We then had six losses, three draws, and just one win before we played Blackburn Rovers at Ewood Park on 24th October. The game ended 1-1 but for me it was remarkable for two reasons. Firstly the goal Blackburn scored was from the penalty spot; Scott Sellars got it past me after a controversial handball decision. Nicky Law was judged to have touched the ball with his hand but he claimed, and I have to say I agreed with him, that it was purely accidental after he was pushed by Colin Hendry. Our manager Dave Smith was fuming. Scott didn't fall for my psychology anyway, and I dived the wrong way. The other reason it was remarkable was that despite not winning I had a great game, making a lot of quality saves from Simon Garner which drew comment from the Blackburn manager Don Mackay, himself a former goalkeeper who said, 'Why is it all these visiting goalkeepers come here and look like they should be playing in the First Division? Surely they can't all be that good? Then you have to start asking some questions about your own strikers.' Praise indeed from the manager of the opposition.

Three losses, a win and a draw followed before we took on Oldham Athletic at Boundary Park. Tommy Tynan scored for us, the only goal of the game, ending 1-0. Not that I wasn't busy because I was. Oldham created fifteen corners to our three, and I kept out chances by Tommy Wright time and again, the last of which was a diving save at full stretch.

In the Shrewsbury game on 5th December I was deemed to have fouled Mickey Brown by grabbing and pulling him down just outside the penalty area. It was described by press reporter Dave Wharton as 'a professional foul.' It all happened in the heat of the moment and to be honest I don't remember much about it now. I hate goalmouth scrambles, as do most goalkeepers, because they very often involve some unavoidable pushing, shoving and pulling while all the time the ball can easily disappear. You can get seventeen or eighteen players in the penalty area sometimes and I often practise it in training. The best goalkeepers in such situations were Pat Jennings with his shovel-like hands, and the 1966 England World Cup winner Gordon Banks. Their timing was always superb. You have to act decisively too, commit to a move and stick to it. In this instance the resulting free kick was deflected off the wall of players and we won the game 2-0.

A goalkeeper has to be tough or the opposition will sense weakness and be all over you. Diving at a man's studded, running boots to get hold of a ball is not for the faint hearted, so you have to be bold on occasion, pouncing like a cat when the time is right. Such timing is everything, because a split second out and you could give away a penalty or even risk getting sent off. But you have to reduce the amount of space the opposition has available to take his shot, while trying not to think of his boot connecting with your face. Avoiding committing a foul is a consideration, but you can't let that worry you so much you don't get stuck in. I've never considered myself to be a 'dirty' player. I think in my worst season I notched up 18 points, with 3 points per foul and 21 leading to a ban. I was standing my ground, literally, but what's most important is I never maliciously hurt anyone doing it.

By this time, mid-season, we were beginning to win more than we were losing. I'd finally found my confidence at Plymouth and was developing a good rapport with the fans, and about time too. In the Birmingham City game on Boxing Day I was forced to keep out several quick fire shots from Gary Childs and Julian Dicks until in the 63rd minute when Tommy Tynan put us ahead from the penalty spot after Doug Anderson was fouled. The game ended 1-0 despite further efforts by Birmingham including one shot that hit my right post.

January didn't start well with two losses, but four wins in a row followed, one of them being against Shrewsbury Town again, this time in the FA Cup. Their manager Ian McNeill thought a last minute header from David Moyes had gone over the line before it was cleared by Leigh Cooper, contrary to what the referee David Hutchinson and linesmen had said. We didn't have brilliant luck either when Tommy Tynan missed a penalty, sending it soaring over the Shrewsbury net much to the amusement of their fans. The game ended 1-0 to us when a Stuart Evans header beat my opposite Steve Perks. Ironically our last game of the season on 7th May 1988 was a loss, to Shrewsbury Town, 2-1. Revenge is sweet.

The last few games of the season saw more losses than wins and so it came as a wonderful surprise to find that in May 1988 I was voted Player of the Year by the Plymouth Argyle fans. I was presented with the trophy on the pitch by Chairman Peter Bloom. What an amazing turnaround: only twelve months before I was being heckled and booed by our own fans, and now I was their favourite. Not only that, I was voted in by the biggest margin to date, at 34% of the vote. Perhaps they felt guilty? The nearest second was Mark Smith with 16% and then Adrian Burrows with 15%. I was shocked and delighted of course, and very flattered. I'd battled on regardless of the jeering criticism, continued playing through increasing self-doubt and loss of confidence to suddenly be rewarded with the greatest compliment a club and its fans can give a player. I'd now played for three clubs and won Player of the Year at each.

I was living the dream with my young family in beautiful Devon close to the seaside, I had my own house in a lovely village with two great pubs, I'd just won Player of the Year, and I was happy. So why did I put in for a transfer?

20

We were homesick. Not literally of course, as we had a lovely home in Devon, but we missed our families in Nottingham. We loved the countryside, and we loved being close to the beach, it was all fantastic of course, but there were some unavoidable drawbacks. My parents were by this time unable to travel as far as Devon on their own, either by car or train, and so it meant driving up to Nottingham to visit them or collect them, so consequently we didn't see them very often as a family. I would call in when passing if I could, and stay a night or two when playing in the Midlands, but it wasn't ideal. It was the same for Julie and her parents too, and both sets of grandparents were obviously missing our kids. I was constantly away playing football, which I know is the usual thing for a footballer, but Devon seemed a long way from the rest of the country. I'll let you in on a secret too, if you can keep this to yourself; I'd always wanted to play for a certain Nottingham club, ever since I was a kid, and I don't mean Forest.

With Dave Smith's blessing I put myself on the transfer list in May 1988. I'd been playing well and I suspected I might be able to secure what I wanted. There'd been rumours of interest from several managers, including the legendary Billy Bremner at Leeds. He had hinted he might be looking for a replacement for their thirty-three-year-old goalkeeper Mervyn Day, stating I was 'one of the best goalkeepers in the Second Division.' He didn't follow this up with an offer though. I wouldn't have accepted anyway. I knew exactly where I wanted to go.

Dave Smith was fine about it, but he didn't want Crudge back in goal on a permanent basis so he told me I couldn't leave until they'd found my replacement, which was fair enough. I'd always got on with Dave and he once gave me some advice which I heeded. He told me he'd heard me shouting during a Reserve game all the way from the car park as he got out of his car. He said, 'You've got to read the game more, Steve. You must try to anticipate what the players are going to do, long before they do it, if you can.' Too many managers and even TV pundits know absolutely nothing about goalkeeping and so a lot of it can be ignored, but this was great advice. Even though it might sound obvious, I took it on board and believe my game improved as a result.

Dave was a great manager and had achieved a lot at Home Park and so it came as a shock to hear he was leaving when he returned to his home town of Dundee that summer to manage Dundee United. Ken Brown took over in July and it would be unfair to say we didn't get on, because we did. Perhaps the fact I was leaving caused some immediate friction that was unnecessary, but I didn't develop the same relationship with him as I had with Dave. In fact it had recently been in the press that I'd put in for a transfer and one of the first things Ken said to me was, 'Don't go to the papers without speaking to me first.' I wouldn't have minded but he said this in front of everyone, as though it was a very public reprimand.

When the new season began in August 1988 I was still at Plymouth Argyle. I kept out my old club Walsall on 27th August, making a few good saves to keep the final score at 2-2. We then had four wins in our next six games until the West Brom game on 24th September, which was memorable for me not because I had a great game but quite the opposite. I picked up an injury that I'm still living with more than three decades later. Ten minutes into the game there were several players in my penalty area when their striker Don Goodman began stepping back into me so I pushed him to clear a space for an incoming cross. It was a gentle shove, nothing more, the kind of unremarkable routine defensive move players expect from any goalkeeper. I couldn't believe what happened next. I heard a massive thud on my head and sudden pain from the side of my face. Goodman had turned around and struck an elbow hard into the right side of my head at the top of my jaw near my ear. I went down immediately without really knowing what had happened, just that I was overwhelmed by the pain. The referee didn't see it, but luckily one of the linesmen did. I have absolutely no doubt in my mind it was deliberate. Goodman was sent off. I received treatment from our sponge man on the pitch; a cold wet sponge and anaesthetic spray, and after a few minutes I carried on. There was no blood and no visible bruising to speak of, and so on the outside it would appear there was no injury. I knew differently of course, and to this day my jaw clicks, for which I've been advised it could be rectified with surgery, but to date I haven't bothered. At half-time as I walked past the away team dressing room I heard shouts of 'Cheating bastard!' and worse. Many clearly thought I'd faked the injury in order to get Goodman sent off. The game looked like it might end at 1-0 to us until Stewart Phillips beat me in the last five minutes, ending it in a draw.

I was in agony for weeks. I found out a few days later that Colin Addison confronted Goodman about the incident straight after the game. 'I've known Steve Cherry for years; I know he wouldn't fake an injury like that. Did you elbow him?' Goodman apparently replied 'Yes I did.' Colin told me he then tried to find me in the players' lounge but I'd already gone. I never received an apology, but I don't bear a grudge; I wouldn't after all these years. Besides, in a way it's part of the game, sports injuries happen, tempers flare, and people make mistakes. It is part of the endless debate surrounding deliberate assaults on the sports field compared to those made outside in the street where the same thing would probably cause the offender to be locked up.

Our house had been sold quicker than expected; a man from London bought it for the asking price in two hours, and we suddenly found ourselves homeless. We decided Julie and the kids should move back up to Nottingham, which they did, temporarily moving in with her brother Andy and his wife Kate. It was very kind of them, and they'd end up staying with them all summer, twelve weeks in total, and so we were both very grateful for their help. We eventually bought a house off Coventry Lane in the Bramcote area of Nottingham just down the road from the crematorium.

Meanwhile I was back in digs at the Santa Barbara guest house in Plymouth. It wasn't an ideal arrangement, and to complicate matters further every Monday I was training at the City Ground with Seamus McDonagh and Mark Crossley of Nottingham Forest. This was a personal favour from Brian Clough to me and the club, and I really enjoyed it. I was still under contract to Plymouth, supposedly for another eighteen months, but Ken Brown didn't mind, saying, 'I'm not that keen on players training with other clubs but it's not quite so critical for a goalkeeper because he isn't involved as much in the tactical side of things.' This is true, obviously. I had only one position I could play in, and so my tactics as such never really changed.

When Rhys Wilmot took my place I was free to move on, though still officially under contract to Plymouth. I began a three month loan period playing for a Midlands club. It wasn't in Nottingham, but it was pretty close: Chesterfield. I'd spoken to their manager Paul Hart on the phone and agreed terms. There was no signing-on fee but £400 a week was okay. It was very handy for me with my family already back in the area. Chesterfield were losing almost every game they played at the start of that season, languishing near the bottom of Division Three, so I was hoping I could help change that in some modest way.

I signed up and on 2nd January 1989 I made my debut appearance for The Spireites, as they are called, named after Chesterfield's famous Church of St Mary with its distinctly crooked spire. It was a good start; we beat Sheffield United 3-1 at Bramhall Lane after we were not expected to win. The goal that I conceded was not entirely my fault either. I'm not being churlish in saying that, Tony Garner blatantly cheated. He clearly palmed it into the net in a deliberate handball just like Diego Maradona in the 1986 World Cup. It's on video. It wasn't a 'Hand of God' this time, more like a 'Hand of Bollocks.' Sadly the referee and linesmen didn't see it so the goal stood. This was a perfect example for the video assistant referee system!

I probably made one of my best saves ever while playing for the Spireites, if you consider a goalkeeper stopping the ball from entering the net when it looked as though it would definitely go in, then this must be one of my top five. It was in the same debut game. The ball had been kicked towards my net and was deflected over my head from one of our defenders as I stood quite far out with my back to the goal. I knew I couldn't back-pedal fast enough so I turned around and ran. Even to me it looked unlikely I would get to the ball in time as it soared overhead towards the open goal, but I remember thinking *just have a go at it*. So I did. With inches to spare I got a touch to the ball with my fingertips as I dived forwards, just enough to deflect it away to the side, missing the goal, right in front of the United fans. I really did *pull a worldy out my arse,* which is footballing vernacular for producing a world-class save. Years later in Menorca I met an elderly gent from Sheffield who recognised me and said 'Do you remember that save when…' I stopped him and said 'I know which one you mean,' knowing straight away he was thinking of this one. He was.

The Spireites didn't have their own training ground at the time and so we trained at local schools and colleges and so on. Maybe because I was the most experienced – and the oldest! – I would organise the warm-up sessions before the rest of the team arrived. I quickly developed a great rapport with my team-mates and they didn't seem to mind me imparting all my knowledge and ideas on them. One of my ideas was a bit of fun and an incentive to play well; an old yellow Plymouth goalkeeping jersey of mine was given to the worst player in training, decided on by general consensus. I'd written 'WORST PLAYER IN

TRAINING' on the back in black felt pen. Listed underneath would be the names of the previous recipients, as the list grew ever longer. On one particular day Chris McMenemy's name was bottom of the list as the last winner. Manager Paul Hart had joined us for a while in a kick-about during the five-a-side training session and for a joke I wrote his name at the bottom. The previous winner had the honour of presenting the yellow jersey to the latest recipient, so Chris and I trotted off upstairs to Paul's office. He was on the phone. He looked at us, saying 'Hang on a minute, lads…' as we held it up towards him at the door, his name clearly visible.

The next few seconds became something of a blur. When you see extreme violence on the TV or in films it all seems quite slow and staged compared to the real thing when it happens right in front of you, very sudden and over in a few seconds. I heard Paul shout 'Don't you dare give me that fucking jersey!' as he ran straight across the office like an Exocet missile. He grabbed hold of Chris, immediately fixing an arm around his neck in a tight head-lock and then he ran forwards with him, both together, and smacked his head so hard against the door he dented it. The door I mean. Maybe Chris's head too, I don't know. I didn't stay to find out; I was off, running down the corridor by this time. I know you're not supposed to leave a man behind in battle, but nothing compares to the wrath of a football manager in full swing!

Half an hour later at the training ground Paul turned up in his car. I thought I was done for. He would surely sack me, or worse. He might even grab me in one of his special Hart head-locks and bash my head against his car door. Should I stand my ground and fight, or should I start running? I watched closely as he got out his car revealing to my amazement that he was actually wearing the yellow jersey, with his name still on the bottom. He didn't mention it at all. In fact nothing more was said about it. If they haven't replaced the door to the manager's office at Chesterfield FC since 1989, you now know what caused the dent in the wood, just about halfway up, in the middle.

By this time we were winning more than we were losing, and I was having a great time at Chesterfield. I met one of my heroes Emlyn Hughes when he visited for a few days during the making of a football documentary, and in all seriousness I was getting on really well with Paul and the other players. I also enjoyed a lot of great support from the fans too. My final game for The Spireites was on 11th February 1989 at Saltergate, against Notts County. We beat them 3-0. Why was it my final game for the Spireites? Because I didn't know it at the time but in less than a week I would be playing for Notts County.

21

Neil Warnock watched me keep a clean sheet against Notts County for the Spireites that Saturday. This particular football manager and chiropodist had only recently moved to Meadow Lane from Scarborough, a wise decision made by Notts Chairman Derek Pavis. On the following Tuesday I had a phone call from Plymouth Argyle giving me permission to speak to Notts County. They also mentioned, almost in passing, that they'd just accepted £70,000 for me from Notts County, and could I pay them a visit for contract talks.

I put on my best suit and drove down to Meadow Lane to see Neil at six o'clock that night. He was pleased to see me, and made me very welcome in his office. We sat and talked for a while before he touched on the initial details of the offer he was willing to make me, and I was surprised at how little he was offering. I wondered if he knew how much I wanted to join Notts County and was gambling on this, but his offer was so poor I thought he was taking the piss at first. I'd recently taken on a bigger mortgage to live in Nottingham and I needed every penny. Football is a business of course, and as a manager you try to get what you want for as little as possible, I do realise this. He said he couldn't offer anything more, the club wouldn't allow it, but most importantly the chairman wouldn't allow it, as I'd already cost them £70,000.

I was very disappointed. Should I take it anyway, just to play for the club? I thought of my family and decided to stand my ground. There were already some huge sums being passed around for other players, not massive by today's standards of course, but bigger than the nothing-at-all I was being offered. He knew I was about to walk out and I even moved towards the door, knowing I was serous, when he stopped me. 'Hang on, I'll ring the chairman,' he said. I thought this might be a dummy phone call, a closing ploy double-glazing salesman often use in order to clinch a deal, but it wasn't. He was nodding his head, looking at me, smiling, ending the phone call with 'Okay, see you in a few minutes.'

I followed him out the door and down into the car park. 'Follow me,' Neil said, as he sped away in his car. Ten minutes later we pulled up outside a nice house in a great area of Nottingham where Chairman Derek Pavis answered the door, immediately smiling, shaking hands and ushering us both inside. His wife Vivian was there, making the drinks, and we sat together in his lounge exchanging pleasantries for a while until Derek and Neil began talking about Notts County's Five Year Plan, the targets, goals, staff, turnover and promotion, all very detailed, like Stalin's plan for the next workers' co-operative. I was drifting a bit until I saw they were looking at me intently, just before Derek said '…and we want you to be part of it, Steve.'

I saw genuine passion for Notts County from both men, and I knew there could be some very interesting times ahead for the club. In the next moment, when they made me an offer I simply couldn't refuse, I knew I was in. I didn't need any more persuasion to join the boyhood club of my dreams, and so we shook hands on a verbal offer. They added some sweeteners too; I'd also get occasional match bonuses and goalkeeper's clean sheet bonuses, full membership of Nottingham's Springwater Golf Club, and a brand new sponsored Ford Escort from Central Motors, the local Ford dealership in Hucknall. Notts County was the first club I'd tried for when I was a kid and I was turned down, but now I'd done it.

I drove away from Meadow Lane very excited and with an incredibly strong urge to celebrate. I thought about ringing my mum and dad, as I knew they'd be pleased, but firstly I drove to my brother-in-law Andy's house and said to him 'You'll never guess who I've just signed for,' followed by 'get your coat, we're going out to celebrate.'

When I arrived home later I couldn't help notice another car on the driveway. It wasn't just on the street outside my house either, but actually on the driveway. I suspected whose car it was, and my suspicions were confirmed when I walked in. Paul Hart and Chris McMenemy were sitting on the sofa in my lounge. How on earth did they know? I hadn't even told my mum and dad yet. Clearly someone had tipped them off.

'I hear you've had talks with Neil?' Paul said, clearly angry. What could I do? I had to be honest from the outset, so I took a deep breath.

'Before you start,' I said, 'it came straight out of the blue,' I said, staring at them, with both hands raised in a classic defensive manner, like I was showing off a new pair of gloves. I thought there might be trouble, but I certainly didn't want any. There was an awkward silence for a moment but thankfully that became the worst of it. There was no shouting or recriminations. Instead we discussed the matter quite calmly. They couldn't match the terms I'd been offered and they knew I'd always wanted to play for Notts County, so in the end we parted on good terms.

It doesn't pay to fall out with people in football, as in any walk of life, because you just never know when you might bump into them again. During my last game with Chesterfield one of the Notts County players Ian McParland (nick name Charlie) was pushing Tony Brien around as he walked off the pitch so I pushed him back. You look after your own players and Tony being shoved around like that incensed me. I thought nothing of it until only a few days later of course when I was in the Notts County dressing room as a County player. Someone shouted 'Where's Charlie' in my direction, but I'm pleased to say nothing happened. Ian and a few others left not long after that anyway.

My first contract with Notts County dated 16th February 1989 stated I was to be paid £425 a week rising in consecutive years to £450 and then £475, with a signing-on fee of £6,666. My second formal contract was a one-page blank proforma document with the gaps filled in with a typewriter. My basic wage was then £600 a week from 1st September 1991 to 30th June 1992, rising to £630 the following year, £660 the year after and £690 a week up to the end of June 1995.

£600 a week was more than twice the current national average wage. In addition I was then paid a signing-on fee of £90,000 divided into four equal instalments of £22,500 in 1991, then the same in 1992, 1993 and 15th October 1994. It was all subject to income tax of course. Clause three was the relegation clause, which I paid little attention to; it stated my weekly salary would drop to £475 if we were relegated. My contract also stated: *The player must provide his own playing/training footwear and gloves during the term of this contract.* Luckily I was sponsored most of the time but I did buy some of it myself. Some clubs provided kit but usually it was just a token gesture of a couple of pairs of gloves a year. Right from the beginning of my career I realised this could become an issue because in heavy training I could easily get through a pair of gloves in a week, and boots every few weeks. When I was seventeen and still at Derby I contacted Puma and simply asked if they had any boots, for promotional reasons. My heroes Gordon Banks and Peter Shilton always wore Pumas, so I thought I'd follow them. I know it was a bit cheeky asking for free stuff, but they not only sent me one pair of boots but from then on they sent me boots on a regular basis whenever I wanted them and I never had to buy a pair again. Several years later while still playing for Notts County my son Jonathan was the mascot for a game against Derby County and he didn't have any kit, so I rang ex-Man Utd player Martin Buchan, now working at Puma. He very kindly sent me a pair of Puma King Stud boots, a track suit, shirts, shorts, socks and a coach's coat. Martin now works for the PFA, the Professional Footballer's Association, in Manchester. I did the same with Sondico; I rang asking if they had any gloves and they sent me a box containing six pairs. I only had to ask and they did this for me several times a year. In return whenever the press were around I'd make sure they could see the label and my Puma boots too of course!

I was Neil Warnock's first signing at Notts County, he'd only been there a few weeks himself. I was followed by Charlie Palmer from Derby County, with others such as Phil Turner and Donal O'Riordan. Neil was organising his team around him, just as he wanted it. He would later confide in me as to how he decided who to keep and who to let go; it wasn't just about performance on the pitch, he said for him it was also about eye contact. In team meetings if a player kept his head down, rarely looking up at him while he was talking, it meant there was no contact between them, in more ways than one. If they weren't playing well or making a decent contribution, these would be gone.

From August 1988 until February 1989 before Neil's arrival Notts County won just nine games out of thirty-six, a truly dreadful record. Neil was determined to change this as soon as possible, and it showed. Saturday 11th February was Mick Leonard's last appearance between the Notts County sticks. This was the game against Chesterfield in which I was in goal for the Spireites and we won 3-0. My first appearance for The Magpies was the following week on 18th February away at Chester City. I had a good game, and I made a few good saves despite losing 1-0. Their goal was a top corner header I could do little to stop, witnessed by a paltry Sealand Road crowd of just 3,165.

Neil was always there, giving us the motivation and encouragement, and his enthusiasm was infectious. We won the next four games, with three of them being clean sheets for me. In fact of the remaining eighteen games of the season we lost just four, in a near complete reversal of fortune. We did so well we narrowly missed the play-offs. The last game on 13th May was at Gillingham and on the way home my brother Bob had asked me if I'd ask the coach driver to take us straight to The Cross Keys pub at Epperstone, just north of Nottingham to celebrate. We knew there would be a lot of County fans there and to their credit the driver and twenty of the twenty-four on the coach agreed. The pub laid on a buffet for us and later we all took cabs into Nottingham, straight to The Black Orchid nightclub. At least that's what I think we did; my memory is a bit hazy after that.

The new season began on 19th August 1989 when we played away at Leyton Orient, to a crowd of 5,000. We won 1-0. We then lost to Shrewsbury Town 3-0 in the League Cup. This hurt, and so it was good to see us beat them 3-1 a week later, even though on aggregate we had still lost overall, 4-3. We lost 1-0 to Blackpool in August but then *of the next twenty-two games of 1989 we were to lose just three.* Both on and off the pitch it was obvious the team were working really well together.

On 30th September our coach broke down on the way back from a 0-0 draw at Swansea City. We were somewhere near Ross-on-Wye and were told it would take at least two hours for a replacement coach to arrive. Tommy Johnson stood up and said, 'Right, I know a great pub near here, anyone coming with me?' He jumped out the door and started walking. We all followed. Half a mile later we found a pub, though I suspect probably not the one he had in mind, but it didn't matter. We decided to stay for a while, like a bunch of mates on a stag weekend. Five pints later we climbed aboard the replacement coach and carried on.

It was around this time that Notts County took on a new physio. I'd not met him before, or even noticed him hanging around the top corridors of Meadow Lane before our first encounter in Nottingham's Colwick Woods. After our usual stretching exercises outside Colwick Race Course we all walked across the road and through the gate into the woods. We ran up the steep hill into the trees for ten minutes before stopping in a clearing where we found the gaffer, Neil, standing with this unknown man in a t-shirt and shorts. 'Morning lads,' Neil said to us, 'I'd like you to meet the new physio, Dave Wilson. Over to you, Dave.'

Dave looked at us in turn before he began.

'F…f…f…f…f…f…f…f…f…f…f…f…f…f…' He paused. We all looked at one another. What the hell was going on? The man carried on.

'F…f…f…f…f…f…f…f…f…f…f…f…f…f…f…firstly, we'll st…st…start with some stretches…'

None of us knew Dave and so we had no idea he had such a terrible stammer. It was very unfair on him to drop in cold like this, without warning. It was funny in those days of course, but out of respect for him and Neil none of us laughed out loud, despite many of us wanting to, like naughty schoolboys in class. It was a poor start for Dave who went on to become very popular. He was also very good at his job. He could loosen you up with a twist of the neck and back massages that were quite incredible. He often went canoeing along the Trent when he had a hangover in order to help him recover, with his dog Bess running along beside him on the bank. He soon acquired the affectionate nickname 'Willow,' which stuck with him for his entire time at Notts County.

Of the four losses we had in the first few months of the season some really hurt; 1-0 to Doncaster Rovers in the FA Cup, 1-0 to Crewe Alexandra, and 4-0 to Bury, at Meadow Lane. The only explanation is other teams have good days when they are on form that obviously coincide with your own temporary lack of form. If we knew the specific reasons we could bottle it and make a fortune. But these were more painful because in 1990 we had become so used to winning. *From March to the end of May that year we didn't lose a single game; fifteen consecutive games without loss,* a truly enviable record. I'd never experienced anything like it, and neither had anyone else on the team.

Our last game of the season on 27th May 1990 was very important, to say the least. It was the play-off final against Tranmere Rovers at Wembley Stadium, to 30,000 people, 15,000 of them reputed to be County fans. It was Notts County's first trip to Wembley in its entire history, and it was a long history; it's the oldest League club in the world, having been established in 1862.

Unlike us, Tranmere Rovers had been to Wembley before; in fact it was only a week before, when Neil had taken us all to watch the game. On 20th May they beat Bristol Rovers 2-1 in the Leyland Daf League Trophy Final, a competition for Third and Fourth Division teams. Ian Muir and Jim Steel scored their goals in front of a massive crowd of 48,000. So they were still on a high, and familiar with the stadium, and winning, but to us it was an entirely new and exciting experience.

As soon as the game began I think it's fair to say we dominated play. We knew we couldn't afford to give Tranmere any chances and so we closed them down as much as possible. You can tell when the game is going your way and this was reinforced when our Tommy Johnson, still only nineteen, scored in the 21st minute. He struck with a low left foot shot from twelve yards out following a perfectly placed cross from Kevin Bartlett, easily beating my opposite Eric Nixon. In the 24th minute I saved a shot from Chris Malkin after he intercepted a dodgy long back-pass from Nicky Platnauer (back passes!), but we still went into half-time at 1-0. We were all upbeat in the dressing room. We dared to believe we would come away from Wembley with a win, even though with only one goal it was still anyone's game. We must get another, just to make it safe.

We ran back onto the immaculately manicured turf to the fantastic sound of our fans chanting 'Super Notts super Notts!' almost completely drowning out the Tranmere fans. Their team's half-time manager talk from John King must have been inspiring because they came at us with renewed vigour, forcing a tip-over save from me in the 59th minute from a Mark Hughes header. Three minutes later we took it back to them; Tommy Johnson's free kick from the left beyond their far post found Craig Short who knocked it into their net at the near post, via a slight touch from Eric Nixon. From then on we didn't give them a chance and closed them down completely until the final whistle blew at 2-0. It was a great team performance.

The Match Ball was presented to our captain Phil Turner in the dressing room by the referee Roger Milford, and Neil said to the press: 'It's a marvellous day for us. Everybody did their job, it was a good all round performance.' He also said 'Steve Cherry pulled off a great save,' referring to the Mark Hughes header. I thoroughly enjoyed the game, and it was nice to be acknowledged by the gaffer. The walk up the famous steps to collect the trophy was wonderful. I can fully understand why Phil Turner was a little overcome with emotion, most of us were, myself included. Promotion would mean a cash injection into the club, and was great for the fans. Chairman Derek Pavis was quoted as saying we should now emulate clubs like Sheffield United, promoted to Division One just a year after reaching the Second.

We were going up. I had to pinch myself I wasn't dreaming. A few days later we all flew to Spain for a week in the Marbella sunshine.

22

Division Two would not be as easy. We all knew this, but if anything it made us work even harder. Our fans were with us, and they made sure we knew, as attendance figures had jumped and they were now louder than ever in their support. Neil was even more determined and there was no sign of complacency at all. We won the first four games of the season before we lost 1-0 to Middlesbrough on 8th September, but then from the beginning of December we had a fantastic run of *nine consecutive games without loss*.

There was snow in Nottingham on 14th February 1991. In itself this wasn't particularly unusual but it lingered for a while so Neil took his team for a jog around the city's Wollaton Park, and it all looked wonderful. We did some interval running on a gentle slope up to the large house, Wollaton Hall, and took part in a very informal fifteen-a-side kick-about with some kids. It was all great public relations stuff for the invited local press and TV cameras. We then borrowed some sledges and despite my warning shouts to get out the way I accidentally bowled over the local TV crew, sending them flying like skittles. Luckily no-one was hurt!

Two days later on 16th February we faced Division One Manchester City in the fifth round of the FA Cup. It was at Meadow Lane, and we knew the home fans would be with us. They certainly were. We'd beaten Oldham Athletic 2-0 in the previous round, so we were quietly confident. Bring it on. The game began calmly enough and evenly matched until I had to deflect a free kick dangerously close to my area and then a diving save to keep out a shot from Mark Ward, which was flagged up as offside. A few minutes later our new lad from Leicester, Alan Paris, helped clear a shot off my goal line, after I'd dived at the feet of Clive Allen, with the ball then hitting my right hand post. Minutes later I deflected a powerful Steve Redmond free kick that was destined for the back of my net, which was then taken on the rebound by Niall Quinn forcing yet another dive from me and a double save in quick succession. I hadn't been as busy as this for quite some time!

Kevin Bartlett hit one over the Man City crossbar before the game quickly returned to me again. I ran out my area to block a shot from David White by diving at his feet, which successfully stopped him. Then at the other end Kevin Bartlett hit over their crossbar again and set up a chance for Phil Turner which flew just wide of the Man City goal. Alan Harper and Niall Quinn both hit my left post and their striker Clive Allen booted the ball high over my cross bar. Sports reporter Sue Mott later said of this flurry of activity on my part that I was 'all reflex and brilliance' despite not catching the ball as often as I perhaps should. I'd kept a clean sheet at half-time, which was the most important thing, despite City's best efforts.

After the break it seemed we were more evenly matched again as the ball flew from one end to the other like a game of tennis. My opposite, Tony Coton, was kept busy for a while by Kevin Bartlett and Phil Turner, but the game was increasingly looking as though it would end 0-0, right up until the 89th minute. Gary Lund, who was actually on the transfer list at the time, found himself with the ball in front of an open Man City goal thanks to a brilliant run from Kevin Bartlett; it was out of Tony's reach as Gary kept his cool and kicked it into the left side of their net. Meadow Lane went berserk.

In the last minute of injury time Niall Quinn hit my cross bar for the second time, but then the referee Philip Don blew the final whistle, ending the game at 1-0. Unbelievably we'd knocked Manchester City out the FA Cup. Our fans were jubilant, as indeed were we! This game has to be on my list as one of my top ten.

Three weeks later on 10th March we travelled to White Hart Lane to play Terry Venebles' Spurs in the FA Cup. We were very definitely the underdogs, but Spurs were rightly wary of us, and with good reason, since knocking Man City out of the Cup. Kevin Bartlett caused them some serious concern early on, and then we were cheeky enough to take the lead after Don O'Riordan scored with a fantastic goal from twenty yards out just before half-time. To be one-up against Spurs in the dressing room at half-time was fantastic, and we enjoyed every moment.

Spurs came back at us hard in the second half and inevitably equalised with a scrappy goal from Mohammed Nayim after a deflection off Chris Short and then my right post, a ball I found difficult to follow let alone stop. It was annoying but if we could hold them down to this, then we'd go home happy. Gary Lund and Kevin Bartlett kept up the pressure and Vinny Samways had a goal disallowed for Spurs after a handball decision. It looked like we might just make it until seven minutes from the end they struck their second past me despite a full stretch dive. I was disappointed, obviously, but it was a great goal from a great player on brilliant form at the time, Paul Gascoigne. The legendary BBC commentator John Motson said 'it was planted with such precision that even Cherry could do nothing about it.' Thanks Motty. Minutes later Gary Lineker took a shot which I kept out just before the final whistle, ending it at 2-1. It was a shame we'd lost but we certainly put up a good fight, and we all really enjoyed the experience.

We were out of the FA Cup, but as always it had been fantastic football. The rest of the season was taken up with League games, and we had more than a little deja-vu; the last seven games were all consecutive wins until the play-offs.

I'd been criticised for allowing a scrappy goal by Middlesbrough on 19th May which was their equaliser, ending the play-off game 1-1. It had been just the sort of goal I hated; a scramble of players in the penalty area causing me to lose sight of the ball. It had been a scrappy game all along actually, with Middlesbrough players being quite argumentative and physical, perhaps reflecting the fact there was so much at stake. But it was a shame I'd let in such an easy goal because for the rest of the time I didn't have much to do. It made me more determined when they met us again three days later, this time at Meadow Lane. I was particularly delighted to keep a clean sheet, winning 1-0, which was 2-1 on aggregate. So we were through to the final against Brighton and Hove Albion at Wembley, for the second year in a row. I couldn't believe it.

The night before the game we all had a meal in the Wembley hotel, and Chairman Derek Pavis said to us all at the end: 'If you win tomorrow I'll double your bonus!' He'd obviously been drinking because he was not usually so generous with money, but we knew he wouldn't have said it if he wasn't serious, and so we knew he'd honour this promise. It would mean the winner's bonus would become a whopping one-off payment of £12,000 each. We cheered and gave him a round of applause. Neil then said a few words, some of which I didn't hear, and after the meal I left for my room without saying anything. Neil came up to see me and said 'Have I upset you?' to which I replied no, he hadn't. He put his arm around me and offered me a whiskey. He was very keen to keep his team happy before such an important game, and he was worried he might have upset me, which he hadn't. This was typical Neil. After a defeat which may have involved some poor or careless play on your part, instead of giving you a very public bollocking in the dressing room, or even a private one in his office, he'd invite you round to his house early on a Sunday morning. It was an invitation you couldn't refuse, obviously, and so you had to attend. He knew you might be hung over from Saturday night and would have preferred to spend time at home with your family, but this was a very subtle kind of punishment. Once at his house, usually at around nine o'clock, his wife would make bacon cobs. He would then select a replay on the TV of the match in which you were awful. He wouldn't say anything, such as 'look at that, you were crap there,' or similar. He didn't need to. To sit in the gaffer's own home watching your mistakes on his TV was enough.

Another ploy Neil used was he'd ensure our best strikers remained fully grounded; on one occasion when we were booked into a guesthouse in Scarborough our strikers Tommy Johnson and Mark Draper were accommodated in basic bunk beds, much to the amusement of the rest of us. This was entirely deliberate. Neil would always be honest with you, and tell you straight if he needed to, and you quickly got to know the Warnock-isms such as 'go and run a bath,' meaning you're not going back on after half-time. Of course he'd shout and rave, particularly at half-time when we were a goal down, as all managers do (there are some hilarious clips on *YouTube* of Neil issuing 'advice' to his players), but if you stood your ground and pointed out you'd tried your best or the mistake was a genuine one, he'd back down. He demanded respect but he was also respectful of his players in return. He was firm but fair, as the old saying goes.

There were 60,000 people crammed into Wembley Stadium in an absolutely amazing atmosphere, at least 24,000 of them Notts County fans. Wembley was still very special for me, as it was for all of us, and we were thrilled just to be there. The occasion was fantastic, but to come away with a win again would be even better, and so that's what we made up our minds to do, together as a team.

We put pressure on Brighton right from the very start and were rewarded when Tommy Johnson got our first with a fantastic header in the 30th minute. Dean Wilkins then hit my crossbar in a long free kick after a slight deflection off the top of Dave Regis's head, and a powerful low shot by Dean Thomas was stopped in a great save by my opposite Perry Digweed.

We were 1-0 up at half-time, and after the break Tommy Johnson made another great run only to hit wide of Brighton's right hand post. Minutes later he tried again but this time found the back of the Brighton net, giving Digweed little chance. County fans were all on their feet shouting and cheering, as was Neil Warnock.

Twenty minutes from the end Phil Turner was brought down just outside the Brighton penalty area by Ian Chapman. Dean Yates took the kick which found Dave Regis in an awkward position for the ball inside the Brighton penalty area. He had to make an instant decision; the ball was too high to kick and too low for a header, but he was ideally placed in front of the goal, so what does he do? He jumped up and very unconventionally chested it into the net for our third. Who cares how it was done, it went in, and under the circumstances it was a great goal! Dean Wilkins got a consolation goal past me a few minutes before the end during a bit of a scramble in the box, but it ended 3-1. We were going up, again, back into the First Division, after an absence of seven years. We were ecstatic, as were the Wembley fans.

When our coach arrived back at Meadow Lane to our astonishment there were hundreds of fans outside waiting for us, despite the heavy rain. When we pulled up there was a spontaneous chorus of: 'I had a wheelbarrow, the wheel fell off, I had a wheelbarrow, the wheel fell off. County, County, County!' It was The Wheelbarrow Song; self-deprecating, nothing to do with football, but unique to Notts County, and totally bloody marvellous. Craig Short even had a small wheelbarrow in black, white and gold in his hands when he emerged from the bus, which sent the fans wild.

A Civic Reception later followed for all Magpies players and staff led by Manager Neil Warnock and it was great to get such public support and acknowledgement from my home city. I'd personally had a great season too, attaining eighteen clean sheets, which I was very proud of. It's what goalkeeping is all about, after all. Does it ever get any better than this?

23

We'd sailed through Division Two, but now our first game in Division One on 17th August 1991 was against Manchester United. Who else? We were playing the big boys now. For me it was fantastic to be back at the top of English football but it was still a little nerve-wracking too, playing for Notts County at Old Trafford in front of 46,000 people, mainly Man Utd fans, or so it seemed. This wasn't the FA Cup either, there were no ripples of warm applause from Man United fans because we were the plucky Division Three underdogs, all such sympathy was gone, and they made sure we knew it. For me personally it was not only great to be back but it was interesting too; I was older and in a way I appreciated it much more. When you revisit a place you notice much more the second time around.

Man United began as they carried on throughout the game, showing us no mercy. We didn't expect any though, and worked as hard as we could to make things difficult for them.

Their first goal came from a rather dubious free kick just outside my area when Craig Short tackled Mark Hughes, intending to kick the ball away which on any other occasion might not even have warranted a free kick, let alone a booking. I guess the Old Trafford crowd can be very persuasive to a referee. In fact quite a few decisions by the referee George Courtney seemed a little suspect to us, and Neil complained about him on more than one occasion during the game and afterwards, but the truth is we were being out-played. Bryan Robson took the kick which Andrei Kanchelskis then got a touch via Dave Regis who didn't clear it away far enough. You can't afford to give anything away at this level and Mark Hughes pounced on it mercilessly from just a few feet out, decisively knocking it into my net. I was devastated and had to work hard to keep it at 1-0 right up to half-time.

After the break they came at us constantly again and even though we made a few good efforts back at them they seemed to dominate the second half. I could see my opposite, Peter Schmeichel, on his debut for Man United, wasn't anywhere near as busy as me. Their second came from one of the many corners they gained both from me and my team-mates. Kanchelskis took the kick which was headed out towards their skipper Bryan Robson who measured it up before banging the ball into the top right corner of my net. To be fair, this was a great goal I could do little to stop, and much better than the scrappy first one. The final score of 2-0 wasn't a very good start for us, but we'd all played to the best of our ability against a team on cracking form. My only consolation was that my performance made me Man of the Match, a flattering compliment which I was always happy to accept!

Our next game was at home against Southampton. We won 1-0. Then on 24th August we were at home again, but this time to Brian Clough's Nottingham Forest. It was a lovely warm sunny day and we began well. They had Stuart Pearce, Roy Keane, Nigel Clough, Teddy Sheringham, amongst other famous names, with their players costing twice as much as ours. My opposite, Mark Crossley, was busy in the first few minutes before Scott Gemmill came back at us and hit my right post. It seemed we were evenly matched for a while with a Craig Short header landing in Mark Crossley's hands before it went into the break at 0-0.

Into the second half and we had possession most of the time at first, with several shots at the Forest goal until after ten minutes a Gary Crosby header from a Roy Keane cross hit my left post and by pure bad luck rolled with a slight inward spin just across the goal line towards the other post. It could so easily have rolled the other way, but it didn't. This goal had a massive psychological effect on Forest as they immediately picked up their game after that and at the same time we somehow lost ours. Several minutes later I went out to stop Gary Charles who then kicked the ball straight past me into the net for his first goal for Forest. Not long after that Roy Keane beat me when I was some distance out; he ran past me while just managing to keep the ball in play next to my right post, and as I ran back he passed it to Teddy Sheringham who couldn't miss with an open goal, and also his first for Forest. Roy Keane then got their fourth after a brilliant run forwards through the middle of the field, and right through our defence. We were totally out-played in the last thirty minutes by Forest and it was one of those games I'd rather forget.

We then drew 2-2 against Chelsea, beat West Ham 2-0, and beat Sheffield

Wednesday 2-1; three good results from which the entire team regained much needed confidence. Just before the West Ham game at Upton Park physio Dave Wilson came in the dressing room with a surprising message from the referee; we had to find alternative socks as our away kit was clashing with West Ham's home strip. In those days physios were also kit men and carried a book with all the team's colours for that season, and so the referee had made this decision when Dave showed him our strip. No doubt Dave should have realised beforehand that this might become an issue, but somewhere it had been overlooked. The problem was we didn't have any other socks with us. Aware of our predicament, our hosts very graciously stepped in and gave us fifteen pairs of socks in their current away colours still in their wrappers. It was understood that they were a gift, as they wouldn't want them back after we'd worn them, and they certainly couldn't sell them on in the club shop. It was the only time I've ever worn any part of a West Ham strip!

We had a great game and spirits were high in the dressing room afterwards because of our 2-0 win, and I was chuffed to keep a clean sheet. Suddenly Dave came in with another surprise announcement. 'I want all these West Ham socks back.' I couldn't believe it, and I thought he was joking at first, but he clearly wasn't. I'd already decided to keep mine; I still had them on and was preparing to stuff them inside my kitbag. Why would anyone want them back? They were filthy dirty, very sweaty, and more than a little bit whiffy. What did he want them for anyway? We knew West Ham had given them to us and didn't expect them back. Then it clicked; he wanted them for himself, for whatever reason. Everyone dutifully handed them over as he walked around the dressing room, all except for me.

'Hand them over, Steve,' he said, standing in front of me, his right hand outstretched, his left hand clutching a smelly bag of sweaty socks.

'I'm keeping mine,' I said.

'No you're not,' he replied.

'Yes I am, Willow,' I said.

'No you're not,' he said, moving closer, his hand hovering menacingly in front of my face. For a second I didn't know what to do but then I stripped off in an instant and walked towards the showers completely naked, apart from my West Ham socks with the shin pads still inside. To my astonishment Dave followed me. I stood in the shower in my socks and turned it on. Dave stood there, waiting. He'd seen me in the nude many times before so I knew he wasn't watching me for that. *He's after my bloody West Ham socks!* I thought, now getting a bit pissed off with him. I wondered what I could do so I turned my back on him and bent forward to touch my toes, holding the pose for a few seconds. I saw his feet move while my head was inverted, and when I stood up he'd gone. I can't imagine what horrendous sight frightened him off! He didn't ask for them again. I still have those socks.

We then had two losses, and two more wins; of our first eleven games we'd lost five, which wasn't brilliant, but not altogether disastrous either, considering we were up against the best in the business.

I then signed a new four year contract with Notts County, and Irishman Don O'Riordan signed for two years. Chairman Derek Pavis told the press these two signings had 'completed the jigsaw' for the club, giving it stability and continuity. For me personally it gave me greater security, and it meant that all going well we could see the children staying local for at least four more years. People often forget many footballers have families and children and a stable family life can affect a player's performance on the pitch in a positive way just as the opposite is true.

On 28th September 1991 we played Luton Town at Kenilworth Road on a bleak, damp, and very foggy day. Both sides created chances all through the first half, Luton more than us, with our new signing Paul Rideout making a great first impression, but we went into the break at 0-0 despite Phil Gray hitting my left post on one occasion. Phil kept up the pressure on me and was clearly determined to beat me. He was rewarded for his persistence in the 69th minute when he headed the ball straight past me and into the net. There was some confusion at first as to whose head it was, as he was up in the air with his team-mate Mick Harford, but it was definitely Phil's.

There were frequent calls from Luton players throughout the game that they'd been brought down by foul play rather than fair tackles, obstructed on several occasions and owed various penalties, which their manager David Pleat mentioned after the game. This may have been because their player Matthew Jackson brought down Phil Turner in the Luton penalty area two minutes from the end resulting in Tommy Johnson scoring from the spot past my opposite Alec Chamberlain. It was the only penalty that was given in what was a bad tempered game, ending 1-1 as a result, with five players booked including their goal scorer Phil Gray.

I know it doesn't make any difference now, so many years after, and I know tempers flare during games, but one of the Luton players spat in my face in the first half after Phil was booked for barging into me. I very publicly wiped my face with my shirt but the referee didn't see any of it. David Pleat later said 'If I find out for sure that one of my players spat he will be fined, I can't support anything like that.' There was a press report later written by respected sports reporter David Stapleton about the incident. Dave Preece accused me of 'play acting', denying anyone had done any spitting. I was surprised Dave had said this as we had been mates together at Walsall. I was furious. I'd never cheat or make up such a story, and some supporters behind the goal said they had witnessed it, but I didn't get any of their names so I couldn't prove it. Nowadays someone would probably have recorded it on their phone, but not in 1991. I found it all a bit sad that the game could be tarnished in this way, along with my reputation. I don't know if there was any formal investigation into it but I didn't hear anything about it after that.

We then lost 3-1 to Manchester City, beat Port Vale 3-2, then lost to Leeds United 4-2 before we played Sheffield United at Bramhall Lane on 22nd October in the Zenith Data Systems Cup. It was an unremarkable game up until the end with both teams evenly matched. For me it was a very memorable game because it ended in every goalkeeper's nightmare: a penalty shoot-out. The first half had been slow, with only one goal in the 19th minute, from Mark Draper, sending us into the break at 1-0 up. In the 54th minute Kevin Bartlett sent us 2-0 up. This should have been where it stayed, but sadly we squandered this lead. Dane Whitehouse got The Blades' first a minute later with a long volley into the bottom left corner of my net followed by Brian Gayle beating me from a Carl Bradshaw corner in the 76th minute, ending the game at 2-2. Two goals followed in extra time, a second from Dane Whitehouse in the 108th minute, and our new lad eighteen-year-old Steve Slawson equalised in the 116th minute, sending the game back to square one again, where it ended, hence the penalty shoot-out.

You can argue that penalties are not the best way to resolve a stalemate, and they are not ideal, but no-one has come up with anything better yet. It certainly puts the goalkeepers of each team under huge pressure, and of course we train for exactly such an eventuality, but it doesn't make it any less jangling on the nerves.

I decided I would apply all my psychological goalkeeping trickery. Mick Lake was the first on the spot for United. I unconsciously urged him to go to my left, as that was the direction I wanted him to go. The swine ignored me completely and kicked it into the net on my right. Mark Wells took our first against my opposite Phil Kite. It went in. So now it was 1-1.

Dane Whitehouse then placed the ball on the spot in front of me. I quietly urged him to go to his left in every way possible without actually telling him. He did, and I stopped it. As each player took a kick it was alternately nerve-wracking for all of us, fans included.

Mark Draper put the ball on the spot facing Phil Kite. He beat him. Now it was 2-1 to us. Our fans cheered. It all depended on the Blades' next penalty kick. John Gannon came up and placed the ball in front of me. Would he kick to his left as I wanted him to? He did. I stopped it. Our fans cheered. Tommy Johnson then had his penalty saved. The United fans cheered, but it was still 2-1 to us. Jamie Hoyland came up for United. He booted it exactly where I wanted and I stopped it. Steve Slawson then went up for us. Phil Kite saved it. It was *still* 2-1.

Finally Clive Mendonca came up for United's last kick, and the decider. He could equalise, sending it into stalemate again. Or he could miss. Or I could save it. I urged him to go to my right, his left. I did everything I could; short of standing there pointing and shouting the way I wanted him to kick the ball. He ran up and kicked it precisely where I wanted him to. I stopped it, and we won. Our fans went wild, as did my team-mates. I was really chuffed. I'd stopped four out of five penalties.

24

Our next challenge was Arsenal at Highbury. Just before the game there was a mix-up with the transport and the wrong coach came to pick us up. I'd left my gloves on the other coach and so to my horror I found myself without my most essential piece of kit. Arsenal's goalkeeper David Seaman was also England's goalkeeper at the time and I asked him straight, 'David, I don't suppose I could borrow a pair of gloves could I?' He could easily have refused, pretended he didn't have any, or just given me any old pair, but instead he smiled and handed me a brand new pair of his own pink and white Adidas gloves.

Arsenal were the current champions so we knew we would be up against it, and sure enough I was busy right from the first whistle. Ian Wright came at me relentlessly but I kept stopping him, making four diving saves I was proud of in the first half, taking us to the break with a clean sheet at 0-0. I was proud of the fact that this £70,000 goalkeeper had stopped the best efforts from Arsenal's £2.5M striker. During the break David said to me 'I don't suppose I'm going to get those gloves back am I?' to which I replied 'David, you were never going to!'

As I took up my position between the sticks with the Arsenal fans behind me I was pleasantly surprised when they gave me a standing ovation for my efforts in the first half, which was fantastic, and very sporting of them.

But then once the whistle blew Arsenal just kept on coming and in the 69th minute Anders Limpar made a fantastic run down the right finishing with a perfect cross to Alan Smith which he planted straight into the back of my net. Only five minutes later Paul Merson lured me out from between my sticks to allow Ian Wright the goal he'd been chasing all through the game, ending it at 2-0. Despite the loss, I had a good game and thoroughly enjoyed it, and was voted Man of the Match. David Seaman had a quiet time with Tommy Johnson making the one and only serious attempt at his goal all through the game. I never did return his gloves, which I kept for years until they finally disintegrated and had to be thrown away.

Tommy and I were among a lot of Notts County players involved in public relations and charity work for the club that year. We presented a cheque for £2,000 at The Pelican pub in Bilboro, Nottingham, in support of Mencap, money raised by The Pelican's own football team. It was a great night and it was absolutely no hardship at all to sit in a pub with fans for a few hours. It was a happy, party atmosphere and was just the thing I enjoy. We also took part in a 24-hour triathlon event at Nottingham's Portland Leisure Centre with Dean Yates for Children in Need. We handed out raffle prizes of signed gloves, shirts and footballs, and again it was no hardship for us and we had a great time. Neil made sure we understood the value of such local charity work, as he was a generous man himself. Local pub team manager Andy Widdowson contacted the club asking for any old kit we no longer needed. Neil took it upon himself to invite Andy to the club in person where he was given the choice of some full sets of used but perfectly decent kits from the kit room. It must have worked its magic because they won the local Cup that season in those kits. Andy wasn't even a Notts County fan, but that didn't matter to Neil. In fact before Neil's generous gesture Andy had tried both Nottingham Forest and Mansfield Town, but neither even bothered to reply. Years later Andy bumped into Neil at the City Ground when he was managing Sheffield United and thanked him again. Neil turned to his assistant and was overheard saying to him, 'You see, not everybody thinks I'm a cunt.'

Dean Yates and I visited twenty-four-year-old Notts County fan Tina Shelton in Nottingham's Queen's Medical Centre just before our return to Division One. She'd been involved in a nasty car accident and broke both hips and her right leg. It was a good job she didn't have heart problems because she nearly died of shock when we walked in!

I took Chris Short, Tommy Johnson, Craig Short and Dean Yates to the Nottingham City Hospital for a photo with my mum at her bedside when she was recovering from an operation. There was a great photo in the local newspaper under the headline 'Team Effort'. My mum was delighted.

I had the great pleasure of opening the newly-refurbished youth club in my home village of Calverton, along with the Lord Mayor of Gedling, Councillor Roland Spencer. I won't be churlish and say I didn't enjoy the celebrity status I had at the time because I did, who wouldn't, it was great fun, and if this could be used for good causes then why not? The parents of six-year-old Joe Bailey from Hucknall, Nottingham, wrote to the club asking for a get well card; he was a huge fan and a member of the Junior Magpies so Neil and I decided we'd go one step further. I gave him the shock of his life when I visited him in Groby Road Hospital in Leicester where he was recovering from heart surgery. I was Joe's favourite player, apparently, and so I took along one of my goalkeeping shirts, which looked like a tent on him, but hopefully he'll have grown into it by now!

The club was also contacted by the parents of a young lad in hospital who was in a deep coma. He was a massive Notts County fan and so I went along to give him support. There wasn't a lot I could do, and I felt a bit of a fraud to be honest; he was unconscious and couldn't possibly have known I was there, but I spoke to him anyway saying, 'Come on, it's Steve Cherry here, pull through, I want to see you back at Meadow lane!' I had no idea whether this had any effect until many years later, in 2010 I was standing in the Players' Lounge at Meadow Lane when the lad's father came up to me. I didn't remember him but he shook my hand and said: 'My lad pulled through after that, Steve. I just wanted to thank you and to tell you we changed his name to Steve we were so grateful to you.' It doesn't really get any better than that, does it?

Our mascot for the match at Villa Park on 16th November was seven-year-old Lianne Hayes from Lindfield Road, Nottingham. She was quite poorly with diabetes and asthma and had been referred to us by Barbara White of the charity 'When you wish upon a star.' Lianne brought us good luck for a while as we played well until Dwight Yorke got the only goal of the match in the 30th minute after he'd tried several times to beat me. A deep cross from Mark Blake enabled him to smash it into the net past me. An otherwise ordinary game was made newsworthy by what happened on the touchline; Neil Warnock was more than a little upset with a nasty tackle on Craig Short by Cyrille Regis and shouted the fact across the pitch. This in turn upset Aston Villa's manager Ron Atkinson who walked over to Neil and prodded him angrily in the back with a rolled up newspaper while shouting expletives at him. Two police officers standing nearby had to intervene and help calm things down. Afterwards Ron Atkinson said 'It was a copy of the *TV Times*. I was just reminding him of a programme on the telly tonight.'

We then lost two and won one until we played Spurs at White Hart Lane on 7th December. We were hoping for a win but Spurs were on great form at the time, and we hadn't won at Tottenham for sixty-eight years, so it wasn't looking good! We nearly made it though, as the score was 1-1 right up until the very last minute when a perfectly placed cross from Paul Stewart found Gary Mabbutt who smashed it into my net literally seconds before the final whistle. I was devastated. We then drew one, lost three and won two before facing Nottingham Forest again at the City Ground on 11th January 1992. We were hoping for a better result than our last meeting when they thrashed us 4-0. Our defence was better, tighter, and I'd kept a clean sheet in four of our previous five games. Craig Short, Charlie Palmer and Dean Yates were working well together as sweepers, and Tommy Johnson and Phil Turner were great up front, but we were still missing some excellent chances. Kevin Bartlett was on the transfer list and Dean Thomas was suspended, but we were very hopeful, and there was a lot of pre-match press build up. Though not as important as the Derby County/ Nottingham Forest games, Notts County vs Forest were local Nottingham derbies, and still attracted a lot of interest. 'Cherry ripe for revenge!' was one press headline before the game as they concentrated on the unmistakable fact I'd let in four goals last time. In an interview with David Stapleton I mentioned my mum had been ill in hospital on that previous occasion, but now she was doing much better. I also stated I was wary of Stuart Pearce, aka *Psycho*, and his now legendary free kicks, 'the scourge of goalkeepers up and down the country,' which was very true of course.

The game had attracted the biggest crowd for a long time, as 30,000 expectant fans crammed into The City Ground. The pressure was on Forest, as their manager Brian Clough had been scathing about their recent loss of form, particularly against Luton Town ten days before, when even though they'd drawn 1-1 he described their performance in typically frank terms as 'garbage.' He was right in a way; they had world-class players such as Teddy Sheringham, Des Walker, Roy Keane and Stuart Pearce, so they were in need of a boost, just hopefully not from us.

As soon as the game began it didn't look good for us. Cloughie must have given them one of his better pre-match team talks because they came at us consistently and without mercy. Kingsley Black got their first in the 4th minute with a spectacular goal from twenty yards out that I admit took me completely by surprise and had little chance in stopping. Teddy Sheringham and Dean Glover had set it up and so after that Sheringham, Roy Keane and Scott Gemmill just kept on coming at me, a dozen times or more in the first half, with Forest completely dominating. I had one of the busiest first halves of my career, just managing to keep them out further until we went into the break still at 1-0.

Neil gave us some of his usual half-time loser's advice in the dressing room. Managers don't have a lot of time in those fifteen minutes so they tend to be succinct and direct. I didn't have to mention that Roy Keane and Scott Gemmill were all over me, he knew of course. With this in mind he made some tactical changes; one of them was getting Chris Short to free up Phil Turner in midfield by marking Roy Keane.

This changed the dynamics because in the 51st minute our new signing from Exeter, Richard Dryden, managed to get through and beat my opposite Mark Crossley with a superb header. Cloughie was seething. He brought on two substitutes, Darren Wassall and Gary Crosby, and we very nearly lost it when Stuart Pearce struck a great shot against my left post before the final whistle blew, keeping it at 1-1. I was surprised the post wasn't dented Stuart hit it so hard. We were really pleased with the result, much more than the Forest fans, obviously! I was delighted and very happy with my performance. Others thought so too; I was voted Man of the Match again.

A week later we had some important visitors at Meadow Lane: Manchester United. A wonderfully supportive home crowd of 21,000 saw us hold them to a 1-1 draw we were delighted with but which was probably seen as a disappointment to Alex Ferguson. We then lost three of our next five games. The losses were starting to become more numerous as the season progressed, and dark clouds were gathering over Notts County. The fans tried making light of it by a new chant on the terraces aimed specifically at the other teams: 'You're nothing special, we lose every week!' It was funny but it was hardly a chant to be proud of.

On 25th February 1992 we played Wimbledon at Meadow Lane. For me, and one of the Wimbledon players, it was very memorable, but not because of the football. It was a reasonable game and started well for us when Craig Short beat my opposite Hans Segers in the 19th minute and we were pleased to go into the break in the lead, having dominated most of the first half. In the second half Wimbledon were playing better, and Notts sweeper Andy Williams tackled Neil Ardley in my penalty area bringing him down in what the referee Steve Lodge decided was a foul. A penalty was ordered and taken by John Fashanu, who successfully converted it in the 77th minute, ignoring all my usual hints.

Four minutes from the end it was still 1-1 when John Fashanu collided with Craig Short just outside my area. It was a particularly brutal collision and I saw John go down heavily like a sack of potatoes. It was no-one's fault and there was certainly no malice involved from either player. These things happen sometimes.

I was closest to John and so couldn't fail to notice he wasn't getting up. Craig had resumed to his feet and had moved off, but I knew something was seriously wrong with John.

I ran over to him and immediately saw that he was shaking and struggling for breath. To my horror I realised he was choking. What should I do? I panicked a bit, as most people would, faced with a real life-or-death situation, and then I just did what I thought was the right thing at the time. He was lying on his back so I instinctively turned him onto his side. By now I could see he wasn't breathing properly at all. At that moment I had no idea what was causing the problem other than perhaps there was a blockage somewhere, so I opened his mouth and stuck my hand inside, grabbing at anything I could find, unblocking his airway while patting him heavily on the back. I didn't think to even remove my gloves, there wasn't time. The game was still in play but others had seen what was happening and were now running across the pitch before the ref blew his whistle. After a few very long and anxious seconds John began coughing, clearing his throat in the process and moments later he was breathing normally again. I didn't know it at the time but he'd swallowed his tongue and without help he would probably have choked to death.

Match officials and medics joined us and took over, but thankfully it wasn't long before he was back on his feet. It was a frightening experience for both of us and I was really pleased he was okay. John later said, 'I could feel my tongue slipping down my throat as I was lying on the ground. I don't normally appreciate having a dirty size five glove shoved down my throat but in this case I owe Steve Cherry an awfully big debt.' Thanks Fash, you're welcome. All in a day's work mate. In truth I didn't do anything anyone else wouldn't have done. Amazingly John was able to resume playing for the last few minutes and went home as normal on the team coach.

25

We played Wimbledon again a week later and lost 2-0, and on 10th March we took on Aston Villa at Meadow Lane. We were still looking for our first win of the year, as we were now languishing in the bottom three. This was a game that was notable for its penalties; the one that happened, and the ones that didn't. I wasn't particularly busy, and neither was my opposite Nigel Spink until referee Dave Elleray decided I'd unfairly pushed Villa player Neil Cox despite not a single one of them appealing for a penalty. This was the same man who refereed our play-off final victory against Brighton the previous season, so he couldn't have been all bad. Steve Staunton took the penalty in the 30th minute, kicking it precisely where I wanted him to with a low shot to my right, allowing me to successfully grab hold of the ball as though my life depended on it.

Paul McGrath then blatantly pushed Steve Slawson with both hands in the Villa penalty area just as he was about to reach a long throw-in, which was appealed for but ignored. Even the Villa manager Ron Atkinson later admitted 'To be fair I thought that McGrath pushed their player and was lucky to get away with it.' This probably made up for a similar decision earlier on where Kevin Richardson was brought down in my penalty area but no penalty was given. Perhaps it was balance? It's a reminder if one was ever needed of the power of referees' decision making. We got a much needed point anyway, as the game ended 0-0, and I was chuffed to be voted Man of the Match.

We lost three of our next four games and on 31st March faced the mighty Liverpool at Anfield. Five hundred County fans travelled to Merseyside and supported us brilliantly all through the game, despite suspecting right from the start as we did that it wasn't going to go our way. Liverpool opened the score sheet in the first quarter of an hour when Ian Rush found Michael Thomas who beat me in the 12th minute. Eight minutes later we could have equalised when Gary Lund and our skipper Phil Turner made a great effort only to end with a corner, not causing my opposite Bruce Grobbelaar any problems at all. Sadly this was one of very few chances we created, as Liverpool came back with their second in the 34th minute when Craig Short lost possession to Steve McManaman who blasted a low shot past me and into my net. At this level you can't afford to offer the opposition anything, least of all Liverpool, as they will exploit any mistake ruthlessly. They were doing really well and were at the opposite end of the table to us at that time. McManaman then hit my post; one of four times Liverpool did this, until the second time he did it Ian Rush was waiting for the rebound which he tapped in for their third in the 58th minute. A Dean Yates header then flew over the Liverpool goal, and five minutes later Barry Venison beat me with a low twenty yard shot for their fourth. I kept out more shots on our goal that I could count but it still ended 4-0.

It was one of our worst defeats of the season, equalling our 4-0 defeat at Forest in August, but we played to the best of our ability, and Liverpool were on cracking form, and so there was no shame in the score. Neil knew we'd worked hard and said of our performance, 'Liverpool are the best side in the country and could easily have repeated their 9-0 slaughter of Crystal Palace two years ago. The reason they didn't was because we stuck with it right to the end.' Sports reporter David Stapleton said: 'Keeper Cherry could not be blamed for any of the goals and made a number of good saves to prevent an even easier Liverpool win.' These were great words, and eased the bitter pill of defeat. But the fact was we kept on losing.

In our next five games we won two, but lost three, until the final game of the season on 2nd May 1992 against Luton Town at Meadow Lane. It's always nice to end the season with a home win. Like us, Luton were desperate to avoid relegation. Soon after the game started Mark Pembridge tried two low shots at my goal, first to my right and then to my left which I anticipated and so stopped both. A low header from Julian James following a long throw-in in the 18th minute opened the score for Luton. Rob Matthews equalised in the 35th minute from twelve yards out which gave my opposite Alec Chamberlain little chance. 1-1 at half-time meant serious manager talks in the dressing rooms of both clubs. A fly on the wall would have probably heard very similar advice as both were in identical positions at the bottom of the table. We finished off Luton however in the 70th minute by a fine goal from twenty-five yards out by Rob Matthews who chipped the ball over Alec's head and into his net.

It was great to end with a win; it made the inevitable a little easier to swallow. It was unavoidable: We were being relegated. However, by a strange twist of fate we were staying in Division One despite being relegated from Division One. Those who follow football closely enough will know why, looking at the year. The Premier League was created in 1992 and would begin in earnest in August of that year. Consequently we were demoted, but stayed in Division One. For me personally I was disappointed; you don't anticipate your club reaching the top only to be demoted after the first season, and I know everyone was as disappointed as I was.

There was a fantastic compensation for me though: I was voted Player of the Year by Notts County fans and it was announced on the pitch. What an honour this was! Not only was I playing for my childhood dream team but I was their favourite player. I was deeply and sincerely chuffed. It was my fourth such accolade in four different clubs, and I was really flattered. I'd recently appeared in the Manchester City fan magazine and Chairman Derek Pavis came up to me on the pitch just after the announcement and whispered in my ear 'How much did you get paid for that article for Man City?' I replied 'Nothing.' This was true. He couldn't understand why I hadn't demanded any payment.

The relegation clause kicked in at this time too; a near 20% cut in salary, as per my contract. I'd never seriously considered it, probably because as soon as I joined we just kept on going up, year after year, until now. I was willing to accept it, the loss of a few quid was understandable, the club would be earning less, but when the reality of it hit me it was a real shock. Whatever you earn you always live to your means, and sometimes beyond, and so this was worrying, not so much for me but for my family. I asked others in the team and many were not taking nearly as much a drop as this. I'd missed only one game since February 1989, at Preston on April 15th 1989 because of injury. I liked to think I made a positive contribution to the club, even a very important contribution, but now it appeared I wasn't as valuable as I thought. I'd signed a four year deal and in September 1992 Derek Pavis the Chairman said, 'In my opinion Steve Cherry is being paid what he is worth. He has three years left of his contract with the club and in that context obviously has a future here. It's up to him whether he plays in the Reserves or First Team.'

It was support, of a fashion, but it wasn't particularly enthusiastic. At least I knew where I stood. In response I said I would offer my services elsewhere, and it became known I had done so, but no immediate offers materialised. To be honest, I really didn't want to leave Meadow Lane, and didn't make much effort to go, I was just a little angry at the way I'd been treated. I therefore became known for a while in the press at the start of the 1992/93 season as 'Notts County's unsettled goalkeeper,' as speculation about my future continued. Eventually I resigned myself to staying at Meadow Lane not because I had nowhere else to go, but because I was happy to stay. Sadly this wasn't the case across the team. This was the same team that had climbed two divisions in successive years, and granted was now struggling a little, but if it had been given more time who knows what we could have achieved.

Some players left and some were sold. We faced the new season without Tommy Johnson (sold to Derby County for £1.3 million), Paul Rideout (sold to Glasgow Rangers for £500,000), and others such as Phil Robinson, John McClelland, Alan Paris and Dave Regis. Neil had told the press only months previously that his team was now probably worth £4 million and he was right; millions were made from the sale of these players, much of the proceeds from which went into the rebuilding of three sides of Meadow Lane at a cost of £3.4 million, with ambitions to build a new Main Stand too at a further cost of £4 million. But how far do you go towards building such a wonderful stadium by selling the very players that helped create the team's success? Some improvements were being forced on clubs due to the Taylor Report after Hillsborough and the rush to provide seating, but huge sums of money were being spent. Football is a business of course, and Meadow Lane certainly needed more than the usual paint job, but this was the first time I doubted Neil's and the Chairman's decision making. It was a very important time for Notts County; probably the most important in its recent history and opinions differ widely about it. If you are a County fan, then you will have to decide for yourself whether you think it was handled correctly or not.

26

The 1992/93 season began on a hot August afternoon with a 1-0 loss to Birmingham City. This wasn't anything to do with me, I didn't even play. I'd been dropped in favour of Bob Catlin. We then drew 1-1 with Leicester City, and I was recalled, only to lose to Watford 2-1. We then won 3-1 at Peterborough, where I enjoyed redeeming myself with some great saves. We then lost 4-2 to Derby County in the Anglo-Italian Cup and suffered a 6-0 drubbing from Millwall at The Den.

Further losses followed; *of the next nineteen games we won only four*. I made some great saves I was proud of in the games against Tranmere Rovers and Cambridge United, despite losing to both. In late November I injured my hand pretty badly and realised it was more than the usual injury when it swelled up and refused to heal within a couple of days. X-rays revealed I'd fractured a finger. With reserve goalkeepers Bob Catlin and Jimmy Walker snapping at my heels I decided to play it down as much as possible, despite finding it very difficult to get my gloves on over the swelling. Pain-killing injections were on offer so I took them before every game, for weeks. I doubt very much I'd be able to get away with that today.

On 5th December we lost 2-0 to Newcastle United at Meadow Lane, but not before I made some good saves I was proud of, despite the broken finger. It was another game we lost but played well in. A week later we beat Cambridge United 1-0 while my finger was still broken. I doubt such repeated activity was doing it any good, it wasn't strapped up or otherwise immobilised, but Neil had already told me Bob Catlin was still on standby, so what else could I do?

I kept a clean sheet against Portsmouth on 19th December, making some career-best saves against Guy Whittingham, Paul Walsh, Steve Agnew, and Kit

Symons in quick succession. It had rained solidly for twenty-four hours before the match at Fratton Park and the referee Martin Bodenham almost called it off, but despite this the pitch was in surprisingly good condition. We gained a much needed point by keeping it at 0-0, and I was delighted to be awarded Man of the Match yet again.

On 12th January 1993 we faced Sunderland in the FA Cup Third Round at Meadow Lane. This game would become an important decider in more ways than one. You could speculate as to what might have happened if we'd won that day, but we lost 2-0. This result was the catalyst for change at Notts County. I suppose if we'd won but then lost the next game it would have merely postponed the inevitable. Anyway, two days after this game we found out that Neil had gone, taking his assistant Mick Jones with him. I was surprised, as most of us were, and I'm not saying I agreed with it. He'd worked wonders with the club and it seemed a little unfair. We now had a fantastic stadium, not built from expensive loans but from the sale of players, and the club's finances were in good shape, as far as I knew. He'd taken us up two divisions, and to Wembley – twice – but fear of relegation back down into the Second Division, what was once the Third Division, was apparently too much for Chairman Derek Pavis. Mick Walker, our Youth Team Coach took over, supposedly on a temporary basis. Neil was very proud of his achievements at Meadow Lane, and with justification, he was a great manager. But that's football. You're only as good as your last game.

It may have been coincidence but our results did improve slightly. Mick brought in centre-half Colin Foster from West Ham and former Everton and England midfielder Peter Reid. Peter in particular was very experienced, having started the season as Manchester City's player-manager, and so he brought a huge amount of knowledge to Meadow Lane.

We lost only one of our next six games and continued on a roll when we met Grimsby Town at Blundell Park. We had the game almost in the bag leading 3-1 until twenty minutes from the end when their midfielder Jim Dobbin sent me flying as his boot made contact with my midriff somewhere, winding me for a minute or so. The referee Alan Wilkie saw it and blew his whistle, giving me time to recover. But they got two more past me; Paul Groves bashed in the third of his hat trick that day from a rebound off the bar originally hit by Jim Dobbin, ending it 3-3. It was an enjoyable game, despite the awful weather and getting kicked in the ribs, with some good football from both teams. Mick Walker continued experimenting with the team and paired Tony Agana and

Gary Lund up front for this game which worked well for a while, as did Chris Short at right back. My opposite Dave Beasant was beaten by three quality goals from Paul Devlin, Gary Lund and Mark Draper, and I admit I made a couple of errors by not punching away the cross before their second goal, but you can't dwell on your mistakes.

Our final game of the season was against Sunderland at Meadow Lane, this time in a League game. I'm pleased to say we beat them 3-1, and stayed in the First Division fairly comfortably at eighth from the bottom. To be relegated again so soon would have been a complete disaster.

I was now in my early thirties and for some people, mainly the opposition fans, my weight had become an issue. I had reached fourteen stone, but I was far from being genuinely overweight. Some were quite vocal and downright rude, but I accepted it as part of the game, part of the theatre that is football. Wolves fans behind my goal would often sing 'You fat bastard, you fat bastard!' whenever I handled the ball, so it was obviously directed at me. They also shouted 'Sumo! Sumo!' to which I would show them an exaggerated yawn, telling them I'd heard it all before.

We played Wolves a lot, in fact between September 1992 and December 1994 we met on no less than seven occasions, so I decided to have a bit of fun with them. Just before one of the 1994 games our defender Andy Legg had the remains of a McChicken Sandwich still in the box in the dressing room so I smuggled it onto the pitch in my glove bag. During a particularly loud chanting session of 'you fat bastard' I took out the box, opened it in front of them so they could all see it, and began eating a piece of fried chicken. It sent them into hysterics obviously, and they accepted it as the great fun it was, laughing with me – not at me – and even applauding. As I said, it was theatre, and I enjoyed it, even though in training we were always told to ignore such jeers from the crowd. Apparently two Wolves fans were asked about me, the first saying 'I can't stand the lairy bastard,' and his mate said 'me neither, but I wouldn't mind buying the bugger if we sold Mick Stowell,' which was a nice compliment from an unlikely source.

This wasn't the only occasion I engaged away fans like this. When jogging around Nottingham in training one day we discovered comedian Chubby Brown was in a gym at Hockley so we decided to pay him a visit. We found him on the top floor tickling a pair of very light dumbbells and so I thrust a scrap of paper in his face, which he promptly signed '*With love and bollocks – Chubbs.*' He told us he was appearing in Nottingham so a few of us went to see him.

I bought a t-shirt at the venue and later wore it under my goalkeeping shirt. After one particular chant of 'you fat bastard' from behind my goal from some Bournemouth fans, I pulled up my shirt revealing the Chubby Brown t-shirt upon which was written 'YOU FAT *ASTARD'. It did the trick. I'd probably be sent off for that today!

I was gaining a reputation as a bit of a joker on the pitch, and sports reporter Rob Hallam described me as 'Steve Cherry, goalkeeper, wit, raconteur and failed anorexic.' I didn't mind this at all, it was just a bit of fun; in fact he said I was one of his favourite footballers. But on the serious side there was also speculation in the local press as to whether I could continue in the professional game because of my age. I told them I had no doubt I could carry on until my late thirties or even until I was forty. Why not? In all honesty I felt I was improving, not getting worse. Just like in any field the more you play the more experience you acquire, and in goalkeeping this is priceless. Other goalkeepers like John Burridge and Steve Sherwood continued until they were forty, so why shouldn't I? Provided I remained free of any debilitating injuries I made it known I wanted to continue with Notts County for the foreseeable future.

Publicly at least I told the press we were all really enjoying playing football under Mick Walker, but this was not entirely true. The atmosphere had changed, and not necessarily for the better. The discipline within the team had begun to fade and Mick didn't command the respect he should have, certainly not as much as his predecessor. This wasn't his fault. He was a quietly spoken man who wasn't one to be shouting all the time, but he was a good listener with a real passion for the game.

Two of Mick's better decisions that summer were to acquire Welshman Andy Legg from Swansea City for £275,000 and Scottish forward Gary McSwegan from Rangers for £400,000. Andy was famous for his long throws and in fact he was currently the world record holder, at 44.6 metres. He'd taken part in a Guinness World Record attempt for the BBC TV programme *Record Breakers* with Cheryl Baker in 1992. It was held at Wembley stadium just before an England international game, and he beat Dave Challinor and Neil Thompson. I had a go at this too, on 3rd March 1994, just before a friendly between England and Denmark. A football agent from London rang me up offering me £300 to throw a ball a few times across the Wembley pitch before the game. As a sweetener he also added all travel expenses plus a night at The Park Plaza Hotel in Hyde Park Corner for me and my family, *and* four tickets to the game. How could I refuse? In my first throw against Paul Sansome and Phil Parks I beat them both. Then in my last of three throws I beat Phil by a foot, and the huge scoreboard lit up with: 'WINNER – STEVE CHERRY!'

I bumped into Cheryl Baker in the tunnel and despite not breaking Andy's record she said 'I hear you've got a long one?' to which I replied 'I've never had that said to me before Cheryl, but thanks for the compliment!' in a kind of Benny Hill way. It was all great fun. I took my family to see *Chitty Chitty Bang Bang* at Her Majesty's Theatre that night and we had a fantastic time. Not only that, England beat Denmark 1-0 too! Andy's record stood until Dave Challinor beat it four years later with a whopping throw of 46.3 metres.

We lost our first game of the new 1993/94 season but then had more success, winning as many as we were losing. On 22nd September we played Newcastle United at St James's Park in the Coca-Cola Cup. Twenty-one-year-old Andy Cole made life miserable for me, scoring a hat trick against me in some lightning, slick football. He was fast, and I'd successfully blocked as many as he got past me, but he was always there, ready to pounce on the smallest mistake anyone made. Paul Bracewell got their fourth, and had it not been for a bizarre own goal by their goalkeeper Pavel Srnicek when he fumbled an indirect free kick in the 16th minute we wouldn't have got one at all. We played them again in the Cup, second round, second leg, on 5th October and this time they were even more ruthless, despite the game taking place at Meadow Lane. Andy Cole got *another* hat trick past me, followed by goals from Malcolm Allen, twice, Peter Beardsley, and Rob Lee. We got one consolation goal, but it ended 7-1, which was 11-2 on aggregate and one of our worst ever defeats. Needless to say, we were out of the Coca-Cola Cup. I'm glad there were only 6,000 people watching. Not long after that I gave my gloves away to BBC Radio Nottingham's Money-spinner Appeal. I'll be honest and admit this wasn't entirely due to generosity on my part; I just couldn't face wearing them again! Not that I'm superstitious or anything. Twenty-three-year-old Notts County fan Adele Cousins snapped them up for £55, admitting she still had a teenage crush on me. Thanks Adele!

We were still in the Anglo-Italian Cup, even though these games were sadly not famous for their record attendances. In fact when we played Ancona at Stadio Del Conero in Italy there were only 1,000 people watching. It didn't matter to us; we were still in the Cup, having beaten Pisa at Meadow Lane 3-2 in November, and Ascoli 4-2 in October. We were also still in the FA Cup too, at least for now.

Our game against Millwall at Meadow Lane on 11th December 1993 was an important milestone for me, and it was mentioned as such in the press; it was my 215th appearance for Notts County, and my 450th League game. It was something to celebrate but certainly didn't mean I could rest on any laurel leaves that happened to be lying around. We'd just had three consecutive wins and so a fourth would have been great, but sadly this event was marked by a 3-1 loss.

After playing AC Ancona at Stadio Del Conero in Italy on 22nd December we swapped shirts with the Italian lads as we all came off the pitch. We were in high spirits having won the game 1-0, and they were more than happy to accept our Notts County shirts in exchange. It's a nice custom but many seem to frown on it nowadays. We didn't anticipate the reaction we received from our own dressing room either. Derek Pavis, the chairman, came bounding in, waving his finger around at us in a very agitated state. 'You lot, get those shirts back, we haven't got money to burn by giving kit away!' At first I thought he was joking, but I quickly realised he was deadly serious. I thought this was very silly to say the least, and a bit petty considering how much cash was spent elsewhere, but we knew the consequences of a refusal; it would have come out of our wages, or we could even have faced a worse sanction like being dropped into the Reserves. This was the chairman after all, so everybody complied. They were collected up and taken over to the Italians, and our shirts returned. But just like my West Ham socks I wanted to keep mine so I pretended I'd already done it; I handed in a spare shirt I found on the floor. Luckily I'd exchanged with the Ancona goalkeeper earlier and it was safely hidden away in my bag. I still have it today.

On 29th January 1994 we held West Ham to a 1-1 draw in the FA Cup, but then they ignominiously kicked us out of the Cup a week later when they beat us 1-0. Such is the beautiful game. On 5th February I had a good game at Fratton Park when we gained a point by holding Portsmouth to a 0-0 draw; it could have easily been 1-0 to them because our Dutch defender Meindert Dijkstra was judged to have handballed and the referee pointed to the spot in front of me with great enthusiasm while blowing his whistle like his life depended on it.

Kit Symons walked up to take the penalty. I stared at him relentlessly while lingering to one side of my unofficial centre spot for as long as possible. I could see he was looking. He must have been watching, and thinking about it, because he kicked the ball exactly where I wanted him to and I stopped it.

After this our fortunes really improved. In fact we were daring to hope we could reach the play-offs for a place in the new Premiership we were doing so well.

On 12th February we took on old rivals Nottingham Forest in another local derby at Meadow Lane. This game and its date have since become something of a legend with Notts County fans. The first half was goalless, and I dare say we played better than Forest, though no doubt Forest fans would disagree. Gary McSwegan scored first by beating Steve Chettle and then my opposite Colin Cooper in the 55th minute. (I've sometimes been mistaken for Steve Chettle, but he's nothing like me, and he's certainly not a goalkeeper!) Meadow Lane erupted in jubilant singing and applause, with a very noticeable silence from the visitors.

As the end of the game approached we thought we'd done it until Forest midfielder and Welsh International Dave Philips beat me with a free kick just six minutes from the final whistle. I was devastated, as we all were, except the Forest fans of course, who were happily taking the piss. It seemed we'd have to be satisfied with a 1-1 draw, unless someone could pull off a miracle in the last few seconds.

A minute later there was a free kick to us in the Forest half which had to be taken a second time by Mark Draper on the insistence of the referee. Our defender, Charlie Palmer, a man not exactly famous for his goal scoring record, then popped up from nowhere and scored the goal of his life in a wonderful nodding header straight into the back of the Forest net. Meadow Lane went wild. Of the measly four goals he scored in his entire career, this must be by far the most important. It certainly was to Notts County fans, who would have knighted him on the spot if they could, and they probably still would. Forest didn't have time to recover as the final whistle blew a few seconds later, ending it at 2-1. The 12th February is now referred to by Notts County fans as 'Charlie Palmer Day', and the man himself has been affectionately known as Sir Charlie ever since.

27

Notts County were winning again, and it was fantastic. On 16th February 1994 we hosted Southend United at Meadow Lane in the Anglo-Italian Cup, for a place in the final. They took the lead fairly quickly but then Paul Devlin equalised for us in the 69th minute and at full-time it was 1-1. Extra time was played but it was still the same, and so it went to the inevitable penalties.

We began when our skipper Phil Turner beat my opposite Simon Royce in the first kick. Then their skipper Gary Poole placed the ball on the spot in front of me for the second. He hit it to my left exactly where I wanted him to and I punched it away to safety. This goal difference creates a massive psychological advantage and puts a lot of extra pressure on the other team. Gary Lund then got our second to make it 2-0. Gary McSwegan and Mark Draper then scored, and three of theirs beat me, making the score 4-3 to us. Meindert Dijkstra came up for us to clinch it, but he missed!

Finally Graham Bressington for Southend could make it 4-4 if he scored with this last shot. He placed the ball on the spot with great reverence and turned to take his run up. I gave him as much of my psychology as I dare, but I needn't have bothered, it was all wasted; he kicked it so wide it didn't even go anywhere near the goal. The pressure must have got to him. The County fans jeered and cheered in quick succession. We'd done it. We were going to Wembley again! I was immediately jumped on by players and even some fans as the celebrations began.

As a team we certainly never lacked any prompting to celebrate. On a visit to Prague during this season Gary McSwegan mysteriously disappeared in the city centre. We were all walking together in the street and suddenly without a sound he just vanished in an instant. 'Where's Gary?' we all said to one another, looking around, mystified as to his apparent disappearance. There was no trace of him. It was like a scene from the comedy *Only Fools and Horses*. A brief search revealed he'd fallen over a low wall surrounding a tree and promptly fallen asleep, or was knocked unconscious, we'll never know which.

This was the same night in which Paul Devlin was found with the top half of his body hanging out his hotel bedroom window four storeys up and had to be hauled back inside quickly before he fell to his death on the concrete below. On our mid-season break in Spain Paul fell off a wall at the Four Seasons Country Club, landing on his face and ripping it to shreds. In the morning his pillow was firmly stuck to the scabby side, the flannelette so completely matted with dried blood and welded to his skin it took him ages to pull it off.

On our way back from Prague Paul Devlin disappeared inside the aeroplane at 30,000 feet. He'd definitely been seen getting on the plane and a check of the doors revealed he'd not jumped out or smashed a window, so after a final search we came to the conclusion he must be in one of the toilets. Sure enough, one of the toilet doors wouldn't open. He must have been in there for half an hour or more, with the door securely locked. No-one could get a response and as the aircraft began its descent into East Midlands Airport the pilot announced over the intercom for everyone to hear: 'Take the door off, get him out, or we'll have to abort the landing. You've got one minute.' An anxious steward appeared with a cordless screwdriver and quickly began dismantling the toilet door. He was working on the third screw when finally there were signs of life from inside. Paul appeared with his trousers around his ankles and was dragged unceremoniously by the steward, dropped into a seat and strapped in, still only partly dressed. Everyone on board applauded. Such drunken antics probably don't happen now in professional football, not to this extent anyway, there's so much money in it and the players are now such valuable assets. But it was a reflection of how well we got on together as a group, something which managers know is so vitally important. Today drugs are just as common as booze. I never took part in any drug-taking and didn't even see anyone else taking them.

We were playing hard on the pitch too, because we then won our next three League games, still with ever hopeful eyes on a play-off place. This was until Sunderland thwarted our ambitions by beating us 2-0 on 5th March. But the Anglo-Italian Cup Final was foremost in our minds, and so amazingly on 20th March 1994 we were back at Wembley for the third time in four years, playing Brescia Calcio. It didn't matter why we were there; every player just loves the opportunity to play at such a fantastic venue, and this time we were hoping to get a Cup at the end of it.

It was a lovely sunny spring day as Mick Walker stood on the pitch and proudly raised the Endsleigh League First Division Manager of the Month Award trophy high over his head before the game. Mick decided we should start with a 4-2-4 formation, different to the line-up used in the recent 3-0 defeat at the Hawthorns by West Brom, though he denied this was anything to do with it. He moved Andy Legg from left back up front with Paul Devlin, with Phil Turner in midfield alongside Mark Draper. Charlie Palmer, aka Sir Charles, replaced Paul Cox in the middle of defence with Michael Johnson. Mick made a great football manager quote to the press about these changes: 'I want us to underline the point that English football is turning more to passing and control than biff and bash.' Well said Mick, I've always thought there's far too much biff and bash!

It was our game to start off with, as Kevin Wilson took a great shot at goal that was stopped really well by my opposite Marco Landucci in a great diving save to his right. Andy Legg was in fine form with his super throw-ins, and he made eight in the first half alone, and together with Gary McSwegan the two of them were making a great impact. It seemed Andy might easily get the ball in the net from anywhere in their half such was the power and accuracy of his throws.

Just before the break Stefano Bonometti knocked the ball out of play with his left hand well inside my penalty area in full view of the thirty-one-year-old Turkish referee Dr Ahmet Cakar and linesman only a few yards away, but instead of a penalty a corner was given. This was a really bizarre decision as it was quite obviously a deliberate handball. That's not just my opinion; you can see it clearly on *YouTube*. Why had none of the match officials spotted it?

Not long into the second half I came out to the edge of my box to challenge Ioan Sabau who then chipped the ball over my head towards Gabriele Ambrosetti, who found my open goal and couldn't miss. I was annoyed with myself but had no time to dwell on it because I was busy. Minutes later I came out to the edge of my area again but this time I thwarted Maurizio Neri. We then had a couple of good shots at their goal that were sadly wide of target, keeping up the pressure at the other end as another Andy Legg throw-in very nearly resulted in a goal; it was only Landucci's knee that knocked the ball off the line. We'd been unlucky, and the game ended 1-0. It was a Wembley final, and very enjoyable, but to a modest crowd of just

17,000. No-one relishes climbing those famous Wembley steps to collect the loser's medal.

We lost only three of the remaining eleven League games of that season, sadly ending with a 2-1 loss to Oxford United, but as far as I was concerned things were going great. I was enjoying life back in Nottingham, as were my family, and it was good not to be commuting long distances to my home ground.

The new season began on 13th August 1994 with a 2-1 loss to Portsmouth followed by mixed results of losses, draws and wins evenly spread. It wasn't spectacular but it wasn't too bad either. We were in Division One and in the Anglo-Italian Cup again, and were doing well. But it seemed this wasn't good enough for the chairman. In September Mick Walker was sacked. We were all surprised. I hadn't enjoyed my time at the club as much since Neil left, but we seemed to be doing okay again, and Mick deserved better. So who would take over?

Russell Slade, our Youth Team and Reserves coach, stepped in as caretaker manager; he'd been Mick's assistant for a while and had been with Notts County for a year. I got on with Russell okay as we were the same age, though he hadn't been in the professional football business anywhere near as long as me, and as usual as a manager he knew nothing about goalkeeping. I kept my head down and stayed professional; playing to the best of my ability, but the team wasn't the same, and it began to show in our playing as the season progressed. Of the thirteen games in the last two months of 1994 we won only three, and the rest were mainly losses, not even draws. We were in serious trouble again and at this rate a certainty for relegation.

In December I was dropped for the televised game against Derby County, in favour of Paul Reece. This in itself was not the main issue; it's the way I found out. Unbelievably I read it in the *Nottingham Evening Post!* I wasn't officially told by the club until match day when I read it on the team sheet in the dressing room. What a way to find out! Was this deliberate, or was it simply poor management? I'll never know. But it was the first time in my career I'd been treated like this, and I wasn't happy.

The fans were giving me a hard time too, and were even shouting abuse before the games started. Russell said to the press: 'He was dropped because he was out of form and when you're at the bottom of the league you can't complain if the manager makes changes.' Fair enough I suppose. I was falling out of favour. Maybe it was time to put myself on the transfer list?

Paul Reece and I trained hard together and we got on well, he's a nice chap.

We both pushed each other very hard and I was happy to pass on some of my experience, as he was nearly ten years my junior. I was coaching him I suppose, and I enjoyed it. I noticed Paul didn't attract anywhere near the same level of abuse I was getting at the time and to some extent this actually put me off playing. This became much worse. On the occasions he was chosen above me I was glad. This was a bad sign. Quite often I hoped he wouldn't pick up an injury because then I'd have to play, and run the usual gauntlet of abuse. This shouldn't happen.

In January 1995 Howard Kendall arrived. We knew about Howard of course, as he'd had great success as a player for Everton in the seventies and then as their manager in the early eighties, but latterly in the nineties he couldn't repeat the same success and we knew he'd resigned from Everton at the end of 1993.

We always welcomed a new gaffer, and Howard brought with him a huge amount of experience in the game. I wasn't anticipating any changes for me personally but I was told some bad news when I took a phone call from Paul Rideout, now at Everton, just after our 5-2 defeat at Manchester City on 18th January. Paul informed me that I was soon to be permanently replaced in the First Team squad by his fellow team-mate, Australian goalkeeper Jason Kearton, apparently coming to Notts on loan. Sure enough Jason arrived a few days later and his first appearance was 21st January at Roker Park against Sunderland. I remember it well because we warmed up together on the pitch just before the game. He said to me 'let's entertain the crowd by doing some keep-ups' as though we were a pair of circus performers, to which I politely declined. Jason was First Team goalkeeper from then on until the middle of March.

There's an inevitable loss of confidence when you're dropped from the First Team, it's a negative psychological blow however you look at it. This loss of confidence obviously began with the abuse I was getting and my subsequent reluctance to play, but now I'd been dropped it just plummeted out of control. I was thirty-five. Perhaps this was the end of my career? Maybe this was their way of telling me? What a sad, ignominious way to end. I was in despair.

I was last out the showers one day, standing with my head against the wall deep in thought as the hot water poured over my shoulders and down my back, when Derek Pavis came in and said to me 'It'll come back, lad, it'll come back.' Clearly others could see how I was feeling and what I was going through, a loss of form and serious loss of confidence the depth of which I'd never had before.

But I was determined not to let it bring me down and so I decided to completely dissolve myself in my work. You can do this if you are fortunate enough to have a job you still love; you can throw all your energies into it in order to keep busy and use it to overcome your dark thoughts in the hope you'll come through the other side okay. I spent a huge amount of extra time in the gym and I was always last away from training sessions. Eventually I lost eleven pounds in weight as a result, which could only be a good thing, and I looked so much better for it. I felt superb too, and my confidence was coming back as a result. But I was still playing in the Reserves.

On 31st January 1995 Notts County held Stoke City to a 0-0 draw at the Victoria Ground in the Anglo-Italian Cup. This meant we'd beaten them 3-2 on aggregate, and Notts County were going to Wembley, again. I was thrilled for the team of course, but it wouldn't be the same watching it on the bench. The final was set for Sunday 19th March and I would still be in the Reserves, or so I thought. A week before Wembley the gaffer called me into his office.

'How'd you like to play at Wembley next week?' he said, with a wry smile, knowing my answer before I gave it, 'Joe Royle has recalled Jason back to Everton, so you've got the job, okay? That is if you want it?'

If I want it, would I like to play in a Wembley Final? You can imagine how I felt.

'That's fantastic boss!' I said, 'of course I do, that's great news.' I couldn't believe it. Clearly my renewed dedication and fitness hadn't gone unnoticed after all. I was playing in another Wembley Final! The press were told that I'd said to Howard Kendall 'I've never felt fitter in my life,' which was true. I'd trained hard, lost weight, and was ready.

Howard made few changes to the team, other than me of course, and like us, Ascoli were fighting against relegation in their own home league, the Italian Serie B. The County fans were loud and supportive, despite a low gate of just 11,700, a reflection perhaps of our current poor League performance, but it was Wembley, and as usual it was fantastic. There was much less pressure in these Anglo-Italian Wembley finals, it wasn't as if a year's work in the League was hanging in the balance, and as a result for me they were far more enjoyable. Apart from that I never expected to be back again, and so I was savouring every moment.

As soon as the first whistle blew we were determined to play at our best. Jonatan Binotto made an early chance which I thought was offside, but no flags went up, and he missed anyway, hitting it wide to the right, but it warmed me up. Then in the 12th minute there was a throw-in required on their right, midway into their half after a clearance by German striker Oliver Bierhoff. Andy

Legg was obviously designated to take the throw, and we all watched as the ball left his hands, arcing its way across the Wembley sky towards the Ascoli goal more like a powerful kick than a throw. We all continued watching as it just kept on going, none of us daring to hope it would reach their goal, but it did.

Goalkeeper Albano Bizzarri misjudged it completely; it was clearly going much further than he first thought. It was going much further than everyone else thought too. When Bizzarri finally realised what was happening he leapt into the air at full stretch but by then it was too late. The ball bounced once behind him in the penalty area and headed straight into the left side of their net. Tony Agana was on the touch line and had tried to kick the ball in for us but didn't need to; he didn't make any contact with it but claimed the goal anyway, when in fact it was from Andy Legg and his amazing throw. There can't be many goals scored directly from a throw-in, least of all in a Wembley Final. Our fans went wild.

Ten minutes later I stopped an Oliver Bierhoff header as he was briefly unmarked in my area, which was an indication of what was to come; Walter Mirabelli found himself in the same position after our defence failed to clear the ball and there was only me to stop him as he chipped the ball to my right and into the net for their equaliser in the 32nd minute. This was a disappointment but only gave us some much needed motivation. Just before the break a lovely cross from Paul Devlin on the right found Devon White in exactly the right place, whose powerful header easily beat Bizzarri, the ball finding the back of their net in the left corner. We were 2-1 up at half-time.

A few minutes after the break Andy Legg took an indirect free kick just outside their penalty area; the ball curved around to the right beautifully and went straight into the net after a slight touch from Bizzarri. It was a superb goal that David Beckham would have been proud of, but it was disallowed. You're not supposed to score from indirect free kicks, just as you're not supposed to score from a direct throw-in! The official reason it was disallowed was apparently obstruction of the goalkeeper. We were fuming, as were our fans.

Ascoli were spurred on by this and came on the attack. The ball was cleared away from our penalty area winning them a corner. Every player on the pitch apart from my opposite Bizzarri was milling around with me in my area when the ball seemed destined for the back of my net until Gary Mills cleared it off the line with a cool header before I took firm hold of it. Ascoli would certainly have scored without Gary's quick thinking.

Fifteen minutes before the end our Reserve goalkeeper, twenty-six-year-old

Paul Reece took my place and made a great save just before the finish, as the final whistle blew at 2-1. It was a fantastic game and lifted our spirits from our League performances.

I made sure I was second up the steps to the Royal Box behind Captain Phil Turner to collect the trophy. I knew full well it could be the last time I would be able to do this. It was a great moment. We were the first English team in three years to win the Anglo-Italian Cup, and it made up for our defeat there by Brescia twelve months before.

I donated my green goalkeeping shirt from this game to BBC Radio Nottingham's Money-spinner Appeal, and it raised £60 for an autism charity. Everyone's a winner.

28

On 1st April 1995 I was back in the First Team and celebrated my 500th League game, and amazingly it was my 265th appearance for Notts County. We lost 3-1 to Barnsley at Meadow Lane. There were ten games after Wembley before the season ended on 7th May, of which we won only one. It was clear Notts County were going down. It was the end of an era for the team and on a personal level for me too. I could see my time at Notts County was coming to a natural end.

The club was rudderless and in decline; the signs had been there for a while but I'd chosen to ignore them. Howard Kendall asked me to take part in a penalty shoot-out at Meadow Lane with the England under 21s to which I agreed. I changed into my kit in the manager's office as the dressing rooms were full, and Howard called me over to his desk. He had a magnum sized bottle of Moet & Chandon champagne under his desk, open and half-consumed, and asked me if I wanted a drink, to which I politely declined; I had to remind him I was in goal in ten minutes. At an away game Tony Agana asked Howard Kendall and Russell Slade who was doing the pre-match warm-up. 'You are, we're busy playing cards' was the answer he was given, as they preferred drinking and playing cards to looking after the team. Howard's days at the club were clearly numbered, or so it seemed. I later found out that club Secretary Ian Moat apparently told the directors about this incident which was a big reason for Howard's later dismissal. It was time to put myself on the transfer list.

The summer of 1995 became a period of unprecedented and very flattering job offers coming my way, once it became known I had been released from Notts County, despite there being a number of other goalkeepers available. My agent at the time, Kevin Mason, stated there was some definite interest from a club in Hong Kong offering me £1,000 a week. I was seriously tempted as you can imagine, but after discussions with Julie we decided it was just too much upheaval for my family, so I turned it down.

Scottish club Hibernian were also showing some interest, as were Tromso in Norway. It was the way I found out about the Tromso offer that was most peculiar; I was at Birmingham airport with my wife and family about to fly off to Menorca when there was a message on the public address system for me to ring relatives in Nottingham. These were the days before mobile phones, obviously, but such an announcement was usually reserved for emergencies, and so I feared the worst. Was somebody ill? What was the problem that required this?

When I arrived at the information desk and picked up the phone I was shocked to find out Tromso management were desperate for a goalkeeper for the Inter Toto Cup, and could I give them a ring? I duly obliged and it turned out their First Team goalkeeper had broken his arm. I was extremely flattered they'd thought of me above the many other goalkeepers there were available, and I had a very nice chat on the phone, but their offer just wasn't good enough to tempt me across the North Sea, so I turned it down. I've no doubt playing and living in Hong Kong or Norway for a few months would have been brilliant, not just for me but for my family. I sometimes wonder what our lives would have been like if we'd taken one of those chances.

In July 1995 I took a phone call from Glenn Roeder at Watford. He initially offered £45,000 a year basic salary on a free transfer, but I accepted £30,000 a year and a taxable £15,000 lump sum up front, and so in the summer I formally left Notts County and signed for Watford. There was no ceremony and no leaving party for my departure. I just left. That's how it was.

I got on well with Glenn, in his third season as manager, but Watford was also in decline and he was soon replaced by Graham Taylor in February 1996. Kevin Miller was first choice goalkeeper and so I was in the Reserves most of the time, which I didn't mind, I got on well with Kevin. Again I enjoyed imparting my knowledge onto a younger goalkeeper. If they wanted to pay me to do this and to keep me on the bench during games then that was okay by me, at least for a while.

Sadly one of the most memorable incidents of my time at the club was not really football related. We were in Sweden for some training and a few friendly games when Kevin and I went for a walk just to get out of the hotel for a while. It was a lovely clear day and we had only been talking about finding somewhere to sit down with a beer when we found a small bar next to a petrol station. The first beer didn't even touch the sides, so we had to have another, just to make sure, you know how it is. Then Kev bought us another, and so I felt obliged to buy him one back, obviously. Then some locals joined in and it would have been rude to just get up and leave, so we had another. Then we had to have one for the road, with just enough time to have one more after that, and then another, and then... I don't remember how we got back to the hotel.

I'd played only four games in the First Team for Watford before I rang Neil Warnock, now at my old club Plymouth Argyle. I saw Plymouth play against Grimsby, Northampton, and away at Oldham and thought they needed someone a bit stronger than my old Notts County understudy Kevin Blackwell. Neil had also contacted me a few months before I left Notts County offering me a job at Huddersfield. He'd offered me a two year contract and had put in a bid of £100,000 for me. This had been refused, as Derek Pavis wanted at least £150,000, which Neil couldn't afford, so the deal fell through. He bought Steve Francis from Chelsea instead for £100,000. Neil had great success in his two years at Huddersfield Town, winning the Yorkshire Electricity Cup in 1994 and taking the Terriers to Wembley in the 1995 play-offs, beating Bristol Rovers for promotion to the First Division. Almost immediately after this he resigned and took up his job at Plymouth, taking some of the players with him.

So now Neil said to me: 'Come down here for a week's trial, to see if you've still got it,' so I did. I was put up in a hotel and trained every day with the team and it felt great to be back. I was made very welcome and got on really well with the rest of the lads. It felt like a true Neil Warnock team again, the same way Notts County did in Neil's early days at the club. I had no hesitation therefore in starting a three month loan period at Plymouth Argyle in February 1996. It really was great to be back.

My first game for Plymouth Argyle the second time around was on 27th February 1996 against Leyton Orient at Brisbane Road, and I'm pleased to say I kept a clean sheet and we won 1-0. We won our next three games also, and in fact we only lost three of our next ten games. On 12th May we played Colchester United at Laymer Road in the play-offs, and lost 1-0. Then on 15th May we played them again, this time at home and won 3-1, which was 3-2 on aggregate. Plymouth Argyle under Neil Warnock were on their way to Wembley, to play Darlington on the 25th May.

I was delighted for them, obviously, but why was I not jumping for joy? It was because my three month loan period ended before that date, and so I would miss it as I was no longer part of the squad. You can imagine how I felt. I was genuinely upset and incredibly frustrated. But I hadn't given up. A couple of weeks before the game Neil called me in to his office. By this time we knew one another pretty well, and I knew Neil appreciated straight talking, so I wondered what it was about. He told me immediately that he wanted me to play at Wembley as first choice goalkeeper.

I was absolutely thrilled, and didn't need any persuading! I would have to sign a contract to play for one match as a Plymouth Argyle player. The figure of £1,000 was mentioned but once we'd agreed to me playing I said I wanted the same as all the other players if we won, just to be fair. I said this almost as a joke, I was so sure he wouldn't agree, but luckily for me he did. I doubt very much I'd have been able to talk to any other manager in this way, but it paid off. I was going to Wembley yet again, for the fifth time in my career, and if we won I'd also get a winner's cash bonus of £7,300.

A week before the final, Neil took us all to The Belfry at Sutton Coldfield for three days, starting on the Monday. He always did this as part of his way to help generate team bonding. Golf enthusiasts like me would play golf, and non-golfers would use the other leisure facilities, which included a fantastic pool. In the evening we would all socialise together in the bars and at the on-site night club, the Bel-Air. We all had a great time as usual and I would suggest it could only have had a positive influence on team morale. When it was time to depart on the Wednesday afternoon Neil told everyone 'See you all at the Wembley Hilton, 6pm, a week on Friday.' I'd already made some important arrangements for the day before the final so I made a special request. 'Can I come Saturday morning? Trust me, gaffer, I'll be there.' To which Neil thought for a moment while staring into my eyes before replying 'Yes, okay, but just make sure nobody sees you arrive.' He didn't ask why, and I didn't tell him. Neil was very trusting, and often prone to spontaneous gestures of generosity.

Two days before the Wembley Final I was at the Telford Golf and Country Club with twenty-four friends and other players, in a golf ritual I'd taken part in for five years. It was already arranged long before I anticipated playing at Wembley. I played nine holes on that Thursday and while I was out of my room someone broke in and stole all my golf gear; jumpers, shirts, trainers, trousers, and any equipment I wasn't using. I'd been completely cleared out, at a cost of over £500. Luckily my football gear was in the boot of my car, so at least I'd have something to wear at Wembley. The next day we played more golf and I went to bed early. It's always the same when you deliberately go to bed early because you have something very important the next day that requires a good night's sleep; you lie there thinking about it, willing yourself to fall asleep, but it just doesn't happen. There's no doubt I was excited about forthcoming events, and perhaps a little nervous too.

Eventually I must have fallen asleep, if only for a few hours, because at five o'clock on Saturday morning, the day of the Wembley final, I was wide awake. I jumped into my Rover and rattled down the M40 as fast as I could. Luckily there were no speed cameras in those days, or I may have accrued twelve penalty points in one journey! I arrived at the hotel in Wembley at seven o'clock. I found the room I should have been in and was looking forward to a couple of hours extra sleep. I crept in quietly and to my surprise Chris Billy was fast asleep in my bed, and Kevin Blackwell was in the other bed. I didn't want to wake them up, so what should I do?

I sneaked into the bathroom and shut the door. I poured a hot bath and climbed in. I then slept for nearly two hours, waking up in cold water but feeling alert and refreshed.

We dressed and ate breakfast together as a team before being transported to the stadium. We had a tour of the ground along with the usual pre-match photos and publicity, before returning to the hotel for lunch at twelve o'clock. Then at two o'clock we were back on the coach for the stadium again. It was just fantastic to be back. I was approaching thirty-six years of age and playing at Wembley again.

29

Running onto the Wembley pitch with your team, seeing those legendary twin towers and hearing the roar from the crowd is always fantastic. We'd attracted a record gate for such a Third Division Play-Off Final, at 43,000, most of which seemed to be Plymouth fans. Both sides were playing a 3-5-2 formation and as the game began it was clear neither team were willing to give ground easily, as both defences were strong.

We were the first to break the initial stalemate when Michael Evans and Adrian Littlejohn broke through but couldn't finish it, quickly followed by Darlington's Matt Appleby shooting over my net from a Robbie Blake cross. Michael and Adrian had another go, shooting high and wide, but it seemed we'd made more chances, and I wasn't very busy.

It was 0-0 at half-time, and Neil gave us some stirring advice, and some praise, though voices were not as raised as they would have been if we'd been losing. We just had to keep up the pressure and keep the defence tight. Unlike us, Darlington had won both their last two legs 2-1, so they were pretty confident, and like us, their fans had never been to Wembley before.

After the break the game continued the same as before with neither side giving much away, until our midfielders Ronnie Mauge and Chris Leadbitter began making progress with some forceful tackles. Emotions were running high but Neil was on his best behaviour today; in the semi-final against Colchester he was so busy giving advice from the touchline he transgressed the rules a little and was evicted from the dugout. But this was Neil Warnock: he climbed into the nearest stand and continued watching undeterred at the front with the Plymouth fans.

Martin Barlow earned us a corner kick from which came a beautifully timed cross from Mark Patterson to Ronnie Mauge who was unmarked and perfectly placed to head the ball into the Darlington net in the 65th minute, beating my opposite Paul Newell. Wembley erupted. The vast majority of the seats were indeed occupied by our supporters, it wasn't just our imagination, and they went wild. 33,000 of the crowd were Plymouth fans and only 10,000 Darlington fans. Apparently there wasn't a single bus or coach left anywhere in Devon that day.

Darlington tried very hard for an equaliser, throwing everyone forward, but they couldn't get past our captain Mick Heathcote and the rest of our defence, and they left themselves open in the process to attacks by Adrian Littlejohn and Mickey Evans. The final whistle blew at 1-0, and we'd won. Paul Williams, whose nickname was Charlie, jumped on my back and I gave him a piggy-back ride around the pitch, all of us cheering with delight. I let out an extra cheer when I suddenly realised I'd just won £8,300.

It was an amazing feeling to walk up those famous steps yet again to collect the trophy and a winner's medal when I never thought I would. I was so sure the Ascoli final had been my last visit. It was Neil's fourth play-off success and my third, and my fifth game at Wembley.

In all five games I'd only conceded three goals, and I was really proud of this. It was great to get my faith back from the Plymouth fans and to be part of such a winning team again.

At six o'clock that night I left the lads and drove back to Telford. Two hours later as soon as I arrived I bought twenty-four pints, a pint for everyone, and the celebrations began in earnest. I drank rather a lot, to say the least, and woke up in the morning with a cracking headache, a raging thirst, and an odd clammy feeling in the bed.

I rolled over and discovered a wet patch six inches across which had soaked through the sheets and onto the mattress. I realised immediately what had happened so I turned the mattress over only to find the wet patch was more than three feet across on that side, so I turned it back again. I decided to leave it in the hope no-one would notice. Perhaps it would dry out before anyone else arrived?

The next day after arriving home I had a call from the hotel demanding a £50 'soilage fee'. I advised them they could take it out of the £500 they owed me for allowing my room to be ransacked a few days before. I never heard another thing about it. I then took my whole family away for three weeks on a fantastic holiday to Florida.

On my return Archie Gemmill rang me for talks at Rotherham. Clearly there were no hard feelings from when he once tried to strangle me in the tunnel just before a game, as he was now offering me a decent package to travel up to Yorkshire. If I signed I'd probably insist on a 'No tunnel strangulations' clause in my contract. I met Archie and John McGovern at the Novotel off Junction 25 of the M1 to discuss terms. I was offered £400 a week and a £20,000 signing-on fee, on a two year contract with The Millers, as they were known. In return I was to take up a First Team place at the Millmoor with Archie and John McGovern as gaffers. I was happy with this; my age was against me and so it was good to still have a First Team place in a Division Two team. Archie and John had great success earlier in April 1996 when they beat Shrewsbury Town 2-1 at Wembley winning the Football League Trophy. Rotherham was fairly close to home too, and I had no other solid offers at the time, so in July 1996 I signed.

I was looking forward to the start of the new season when news came through to us at the end of July that John and Archie were gone. Uruguayan manager Danny Bergara arrived at the club from a short spell at Sheffield Wednesday. I knew little about him but the main thing was I was still first choice goalkeeper, at least for a while, despite Danny bringing in goalkeeper Kevin Pilkington.

My first appearance between the sticks for The Millers was at my old club Walsall on 17th August, where we drew 1-1. It was a reasonable start to the season but sadly it was no indication of what was to come. We lost the next seven games in a row. I was extremely busy in all these games, keeping out far more than got past me, and most were lost by just one goal, but it wasn't an enjoyable situation. My voice was hoarse at the end of every game from shouting advice to colleagues, but still we struggled.

I was always very generous with my words of advice to defenders during a game; at Notts County I'd shout 'Win it!' to Charlie Palmer and the same to Craig Short if it was on his side. 'Chest it back!' meant knock it back to me or 'Knock it long!' to kick it down the field, and 'Hold it!' meaning to keep the ball under control. Most players appreciated this and the fact that it was not simply me being arrogant. It was all meant with genuine sincerity based on my experience, and some would often come up to me after a game and say 'great talking, Steve, thanks,' or similar. Some didn't like it though, particularly in the non-league clubs I played for later in my career. One player always did the opposite to what I told him and would chest it when I asked him to head it and vice-versa.

At the end of October as the losses continued, Kevin replaced me in the First Team, but little changed with the results, in fact things worsened; we lost 4-1 to Scunthorpe United in the FA Cup on 16th November, and took a 6-2 drubbing at Peterborough United on 30th November. But it was clear I was going nowhere with Rotherham. After twenty League appearances and three Cup games, I'd had enough, and so in January 1997 I made it known I was available again. I eventually left on good terms with mutual consent, as they say in the press.

The Football Association produced a pamphlet listing which players were currently available. It contained full names, addresses and contact phone numbers, and a copy was sent to every manager. I was contacted by Steve Berry, the manager of Kettering Town, The Poppies, as they are known, who asked if I would be willing to play on a part-time basis. I drove to the ground at Rockingham Road and agreed. I trained twice a week in addition to playing in the games, just for expenses, which came to about £100 a week. I know it wasn't a lot, but I really enjoyed playing and with petrol costs and so on, I was probably making a loss.

I was also contacted by Colin Todd offering me third choice at Bolton, and I was very tempted, but I also had a call at the beginning of March from Brian Talbot, the recently appointed manager of a new club called Rushden and Diamonds in Northamptonshire. I was still playing part-time for Kettering Town at the time, and we were bitter rivals of The Diamonds. I was offered first choice goalkeeper, still part-time but on a salary of £400 a week and a huge £20,000 signing-on fee. At my age this was brilliant, so I met Roger Ashby, Brian's assistant, at Leicester Forest East M1 services. I think they both assumed it would be a done deal before I even got there because I heard Brian on the phone to Roger saying 'Has he signed yet? Tell him if he plays against us next Monday, the deal's off.' This made me angry because they clearly wanted me to abandon Kettering immediately, without notice, so I refused. I played for Kettering as planned and made several great saves, despite losing to the Diamonds 1-0. Two days later Brian rang me again: 'Please come and see us.'

30

The Diamonds were an exciting new non-league club, formed only five years before from two smaller clubs, Rushden Town and Irthlingborough Diamonds and they were desperate to acquire footballing experience and climb up into the League. Nene Park was easy to get to down the M1 and A6, and their offer was incredible for such a small club and for someone my age. Having said that, I remember Archie Gemmill was in the First Team at Derby County in 1983 when he was thirty-seven and still making a positive impact on the pitch.

Nene Park was a good looking 6,000 seater stadium under renovation and I signed in the manager's office. They had a wonderful training ground right next door and it was a very promising club. In March 1997 it seemed money was no object at The Diamonds. The chairman was Max Griggs, owner of the famous Dr. Martens footwear company, and it was his idea to merge the two smaller clubs to create The Diamonds. It wasn't until after I'd signed that Roger said to me 'Are you happy with the signing-on fee?' while giving me one of those knowing looks with a wry smile. I didn't click at the time but it was clear they would have paid more. I've never been brilliant with money, as anyone who knows me would agree, whether it comes to obtaining it, or spending it, and I probably missed an opportunity there.

I got on well with Brian and Roger. Brian wasn't that much older than me and had a great career with Arsenal playing in hundreds of First Team games in the eighties. He was almost legendary and was very professional and always smartly dressed. Roger was a gentle giant and a really nice bloke, though I didn't see that much of him to be honest.

My first appearance for The Diamonds was a home game on Saturday 22nd March 1997 against Telford United. The Diamonds had not lost a game since February, winning the last four in a row, beating local rivals Kettering Town 5-1 on 8th March, so expectations were high. They were above halfway up the Conference table and determined to go higher. The crowd were very supportive, if relatively tiny at just a few thousand, but I enjoyed the game. Even though I wasn't particularly busy I was very pleased to keep a clean sheet, winning 2-0. We also won our next game against Welling United 1-0, drew with Dover Athletic 1-1, and Hayes 2-2. We took a confidence boost when we beat Southport 3-0 on 5th April, perhaps resting on our laurels a little too much as we then lost 3-2 to Bath City and 4-1 to Stevenage Boro. We then beat Halifax Town 1-0, drew 1-1 with Woking, and finally ended the season on a high with a 3-2 win against Altrincham United. These were good games I enjoyed, and I've included all the names of the teams so you can see who I was playing at the time. They were not Arsenal, Man Utd, West Ham or other such big names, but the passion was there just the same in both players and fans and in a way there was a greater connection with the fans due to the smaller venues, as I realised when I played for Walsall after Derby County many years before.

The new season began badly on Saturday 16th August 1997. We lost 1-0 to Northwich Victoria, then 2-0 to Farnborough Town, and then 2-0 to Leek Town before drawing 1-1 to Hednesford Town on 25th August. We had a couple of new players, Adrian Foster and Paul Underwood, but gaining only one point from the first four games was terrible. Saturday 30th August against Gateshead was a landmark for The Diamonds as it was their 300th game as a club and it was marked and celebrated around the ground before kick-off. Some of the positivity from this rubbed off as we won 3-2. Three games later on 13th September we played at home against Farnborough Town and everyone on the pitch had a blinding game in which ten goals were scored, and it was great football entertainment for the fans. I'm happy to say it ended in a 5-5 draw, I really enjoyed it, and it became the Vauxhall Conference's second highest scoring game in its history!

After the game I was summoned to see Brian Talbot. 'Your timing's gone,' he said, completely out of the blue. I was astonished, after a great game such as that? I couldn't believe it. He told me I was to be released, and local goalkeeper Darren Watts was to take my place before ex-Nottingham Forest Youth Team goalkeeper Mark Smith arrived. Such is football. Brian was then quite conciliatory and said to me 'I don't want to be the person who finishes your career', perhaps saying this out of guilt, so he set me up with a few games for nearby Rothwell Corinthians on £100 weekly expenses. But I made it known that I was available again.

I had a call from Steve Richardson, a friend of Neil Warnock's, asking if I'd be interested in playing part-time for Gainsborough Trinity in Lincolnshire, so I drove up to The Northolme in the centre of Gainsborough to speak to Steve.

He offered me £165 a week with no signing-on fee. I know I wasn't in the top flight anymore but I needed something extra to cover travel costs and wear and tear on my car, so I asked for a £500 signing-on fee; Gainsborough was an hour's drive from Nottingham after all. He said 'Sign first, and then I'll give you the five hundred when you start training.' I refused and walked away, straight to the club bar. A few minutes later he appeared next to me at the bar while I was talking to some of the players. He handed me a roll of cash and a one year contract, saying 'there's the five hundred, sign it.' So I did.

It became clear that I could no longer earn a living from football alone. Age creeps up on everyone but a highly competitive career like mine requiring peak physical fitness comes to an end sooner than most. I saw a job advertised for a goalkeeping coach co-ordinator at Soccer Schools UK based in Hucknall, Nottingham. The salary was £20,000 a year and could be the financial stability I needed. I was delighted when I was offered the job and so I took it, as it seemed ideal. It involved some office work but I was happy with this provided I could keep up my part-time football, which was a great release and good practice of course. Sadly this job didn't last as the company folded after just three months.

My brother-in-law Andy Griffin had put my name down at Player's Imperial Tobacco, one of Nottingham's biggest employers at the time, and quite fortuitously after the Soccer Schools job fell through I was contacted by Barbara Cobb in Player's HR department offering me a job. This was fantastic news. It meant I could continue playing for non-league clubs for little or nothing other than expenses, thereby extending my life between the sticks. I would stay at Player's for the next eighteen years.

I enjoyed playing at Gainsborough and luckily I was working shifts at Player's and so I could attend most training sessions, usually twice a week, if I moved my shifts around. Quite often this would necessitate other colleagues accommodating me and it worked well at first. I wasn't in management or anywhere behind a desk but on the shop floor, operating a clamp truck similar to a fork-lift, moving huge bales of tobacco around the factory. I was given all the necessary training and I really enjoyed it, and I had great banter with the other lads I was working with. I undertook that particular role at Player's for the next fifteen years.

While I was playing for Gainsborough I had a call from Danny Bergara, now at Grantham Town, offering me the same money I was on at Gainsborough in order to play for him. This was the man who had brought in Kevin Pilkington to replace me when I was at Rotherham United. I asked him why I would leave Gainsborough to go to Grantham for the same money. I was enjoying Gainsborough and knew the lads there and got on well with the fans, so my answer was a polite 'no thanks.' He didn't improve his offer so I stayed where I was.

After several months at Gainsborough I began to come across problems changing shifts at Player's. Whether this was jealousy or bloody-mindedness on the part of colleagues I'll never know, but as a result of being unable to change some shifts I began missing Wednesday training sessions. The club understood at first but strictly speaking I was breaching my agreed contract by not attending. Eventually they had to get another goalkeeper and they let me go. I feel quite bitter about this, not the way the club treated me, but the way some colleagues at Player's had for whatever reason deliberately refused to help me out.

My son Jonathan was now at Fernwood School in Wollaton, Nottingham, and was playing for Wollaton Hall Youth Team. I knew the school because I called in once when I was still at Notts County and took part in a kick-about with the junior school kids trying to score goals past me; I let one or two in, but I didn't want them to think life was easy so I stopped the rest! I met Tony Grahame who was managing the Youth Team and I was happy to become involved.

We held weekly training sessions usually on weekday evenings but also on Sunday mornings during pre-season. I based these sessions on what I knew; professional football training. I had to remind myself, and I have to say Tony also politely pointed out, that these were young lads and not professionals, and some found it tough. We'd sometimes train at Wollaton Park, in front of the big house, with two cones twenty-five yards apart and two teams, running between each. At the cones the boys had to rest their head on top of the cone and run around it ten times before running back to the other one, with hilarious consequences.

We often had no proper referee so I stood in on occasions, and I don't think I was very popular. I wasn't used to getting back chat! As anyone who deals with kids will tell you, very often the biggest problems come from over-protective parents. I almost had a serious scrape with a dad when I was shouting some of my goalkeeping advice to his son at an away game, and I had to remove myself to the opposite side of the pitch in a tactical withdrawal!

We followed the same lads from aged eight, right up until they finished at sixteen. Some of them took it further; Will Hoskins went on to play for Watford, and Tom Groves for Nottingham Forest. There's a huge amount of satisfaction in voluntary work, as anyone involved in it will tell you. It makes up for all the hours of preparation including having Tony balanced on my shoulders every time we set up the nets, all year round and in all weathers. We produced some good results too; in our second year of managing the team together we won the Notts and Derby under 16s League. The trophy was awarded at the Assembly Rooms in Derby, and when Tony and I accepted it on stage I mentioned that the last time I was there was in 1984 when I won Derby County Player of the Year. I thoroughly enjoyed helping to run this team, and if anyone asks, this was Steve Cherry's only job as Assistant Manager of a football team!

Towards the end of 1997 I was contacted by Mel Sterland at non-league club Stalybridge Celtic near Manchester. I drove up to see him at The Bower Fold and I was offered First Team goalkeeper for £120 a week expenses. The ground was fantastic and I was made very welcome so I signed. My son Jonathan helped me train at home and I trained with the club once a week. My first game was against Leek Town on 24th January 1998 and we drew 2-2. We then played Dover Athletic on 7th February and I kept a clean sheet when we won 1-0. I had a great game, saving a brilliant free kick but it was notable for one other huge personal reason: it was the last time I played professional football in front of TV cameras, and even then it was a Diamond Cable TV channel. You remember things like that. At least we won.

We then held Gateshead to a 2-2 draw, and beat Morecambe 3-1, and I was pleased with the way I was playing, until Monday 23rd February when we played Kidderminster Harriers: Don't ask. They were on form, we weren't, and I admit I didn't have the best game, though as usual it could have been much worse. We lost 5-0. I was hoping this would be a blip and we'd be back on form for our game against my old club Rushden and Diamonds at Nene Park on 28th February, and I wondered if I'd get a hostile reception from the Diamonds fans.

31

I needn't have worried; I was pleasantly surprised to find I was given quite a warm welcome at Nene Park. Did they know something I didn't? As soon as the game began I was earning my expenses. In the first minute I was left totally exposed as Darren Collins came forward with only me to stop him, with his shot thankfully hitting my right post. We were poor in defence again and my throat was hoarse from shouting at our lads as I'd done all through the previous game. They kept up the pressure and I made two saves I was proud of in the first half until a goalmouth scramble, one of the things I hate most, produced their first in the 27th minute when Michael Mison knocked it past me with a low shot. He and Darren Collins kept this up until just before the break Darren beat me with a goal I could do little to stop.

The half-time manager's talk from Mel Sterland was aimed primarily at our defence, which to be honest was more than a little crap. But The Diamonds were on a run of good form and Mel acknowledged I'd made a couple of great saves. Brian Talbot brought on Adrian Foster in the second half and it seemed to be an inspired decision as he shot one past me in the first minute, narrowly missing my goal. From then on the entire game was in our half, and my opposite Mark Smith in the Diamonds' goal was probably bored stiff he had so little to do, except watch me work. Adrian kept it up eventually beating me with a great header in the 82nd minute for their third. He'd have got another had it not been for his team-mate Michael Mison accidently blocking his header on the touchline, the game finally ending at 3-0. We were out-played by The Diamonds all through the game, but one positive came at the final whistle when their fans gave me a round of applause for my efforts, with the memory of the previous season still fresh in their minds. Another game where despite the loss, I performed well and enjoyed it.

On 7th March we drew 1-1 with Stevenage Borough, then lost 2-1 to Yeovil Town and won 2-1 at Welling United. My tenth appearance for Stalybridge Celtic was a good game against Gateshead, ending 3-3. It was my last for the 'Bridge, and soon after that we parted on good terms.

In the summer I was contacted by Steve Parkin at Mansfield Town, having seen that I was available again. His regular goalkeeper Ian Bowling was unavailable at the start of the season and would I like to play one match for £200? I agreed and trained with them twice the week before the game and on 8th August they picked me up just off the motorway on the way to Brentford. We were out-played and lost 3-0, during which time I took a knee to the right side of my face which was bloody painful. This was my one and only appearance for Mansfield Town.

In the early nineties I set up PUTS: 'Players under the Thumbs,' an amateur golf team of like-minded golf fanatics. We began in Telford, then moved to Staverton Park, and then spent eighteen years at North Shore, Skegness, before returning to Telford. Former Notts County player Paul Rideout once donated £50 to the team so we set up our own version of the Ryder Cup in his honour, amongst other trophies. It all went well until some internal politics caused it to fold fairly recently, but I still play golf when I can, very often with Tony Grahame. Golf requires much less exertion than goalkeeping, and so I am able to continue feeding my competitive spirit.

I took a lot of phone calls from various clubs in the next few years including Andy Richie, the gaffer at Oldham Athletic. Neil Warnock had finished a short stay at the club in 1999 and I was offered one game for £200 at forty-eight hours' notice, as cover for the first team goalkeeper in case of sickness or injury. I was between clubs at the time and so I agreed. I was in the squad and attended the game against Wycombe Wanderers in a suit with my kit at the ready, but I didn't play.

I spent three months back at Notts County under Sam Allardyce in 1999 in the Reserves passing on my footballing knowledge to the youngsters. This was probably the first time I realised my future lay more in coaching than playing. When Derek Pavis saw me he said 'I didn't know you were back. I'd have advertised it in the press to get more gate money.' He clearly did know I was back, but I took this comment as a veiled compliment.

2000 was not a great year for me personally. I took a call at five-twenty in the morning on 13th November from the hospital informing me my dad had passed away. They say when a man's father dies he's never quite the same again, and this is true. He was three days short of his 83rd birthday and a few days away from his wedding anniversary. He was a man who never complained and took his problems and pains quietly. On one occasion years before, he sat very quiet for a while in his chair in the lounge at home not saying a word, so we knew something was wrong. It turned out he had peritonitis and had to be rushed to hospital. He'd been in extreme agony but had never said anything to anyone. I never saw him show any emotion, apart from when we were both crying with laughter at Norman Wisdom. Now he was gone I seriously wondered whether I could carry on without him.

I drove over to my mum and dad's house in Calverton to break the news to my mum. She was heartbroken. She was battling cancer herself and had already had a mastectomy and now had a stoma for bowel cancer. You reflect on someone's life and their influence on you when they pass away and my dad's was everything to me. In return for all the help they gave me I used to cut their lawn every few weeks in the summer when I could and take them out for a meal in our favourite pubs in Nottingham, with Christmas Eve walks around Rufford Park followed by a meal at the nearby Rose Cottage pub. Now it was all over.

I became increasingly involved in coaching and early in 2001 I took up a post as part-time goalkeeping coach for Lincoln City at Sincil Bank after a call from player-manager Phil Stant. I got on well with Phil and I had huge respect for him, after his time in the army and involvement in the Falklands War. Sadly this didn't help his football management and he was soon replaced by my old friend Alan Buckley. I coached Alan Marriott who'd arrived at the club from Spurs, and I could see Alan had huge potential. He had great technique and brilliant goalkeeping ability, and I recommended the club should definitely keep him and develop his abilities. I told Alan there was more to goalkeeping than just shouting at the defence and he should call out their names so there was no confusion among the players. He said to me 'I can't talk like you Steve,' to which I replied 'you've got to learn if you want to progress.' He did learn, and he certainly progressed.

At the end of the 2002 season Alan Buckley was replaced at Lincoln City by Keith Alexander, and it was in the next season that Alan Marriott's goalkeeping broke records at the club; eighteen clean sheets followed by nineteen in the next season. This continued to improve and by 2007 after his 300th League appearance he'd achieved more than 102 clean sheets, a Football

League Record. He was certainly a brilliant goalkeeper and huge favourite with the Imps fans!

In 2003 I was contacted by John Ramshaw at Kidsgrove Athletic near Stoke-on-Trent, looking for a part-time goalkeeper. I signed for a full season and we had a great run up to the Staffordshire Senior Cup culminating in a 1-0 victory over Stafford Rangers in the final at the Britannia Stadium. I had a really fantastic time, what I call one of my Man City games it was so good. There were only a few thousand seats taken in the massive stadium, but it was a great game and I was delighted to keep a clean sheet. I only found out fairly recently that had Wembley Stadium been available it could well have been held there, as my 6th Wembley final.

I played in a few games for Belper Town after a big chap called Gary with a dubious coaching badge asked me to join them for a while. My son Jonathan was also a reserve goalkeeper with them and we travelled there and trained together. I picked up a knee injury a week before we played Shepshed away and when I turned up for the game they already had another goalkeeper, a ginger lad with a rather feminine bob hairstyle, and I was told I wasn't needed. I didn't feel this was the best way to be treated so I finished with them. It was a shame Gary never attended any training sessions; it might have been a good idea.

In 2006 I rang Steve Thompson at Notts County offering my services again, but this time as a part-time goalkeeping coach. I was taken on for £500 a month and it was great to be back at the club in this new role. The following year Steve was sacked and Ian McParland took over. Ian and I didn't really get on, after an incident years before when I pushed him on the pitch just before I joined County in 1989, and so I feared the worst. I needn't have worried because one of the first things Ian told me was that he was happy for me to continue at the club. I was coaching Kevin Pilkington at the time and he later went on to become Player of the Year. When a goalkeeper is awarded this title it can often mean bad news is on the way for the club. I've been honoured in this way several times but if you think about it, it means the goalkeeper has been very busy all season, which could be an indication as to the state of the team's defence amongst other things!

Everything seemed to be going okay at Notts County until Ian summoned me into his office and said 'I want you to work the same hours every week on Tuesdays and Thursdays and come on the coach with us on Friday nights.' He knew I was working shifts at Player's and couldn't possibly do it. He wanted me to leave my well-paid full-time employment at Player's for a £500 a month coaching job. This was his way of getting rid of me. I called his bluff and said 'yes'. I then went on holiday for three weeks with my family. A few days later I had a call while sitting on the beach in Menorca. It was Dean Yates. He said to me 'You'll never guess who's coming to Notts County.' I immediately replied 'Mick Leonard.' Dean said 'How the hell did you know that?' I knew because Mick and Ian were best friends. When I came back from Menorca I didn't return to Notts County, I just didn't go there anymore, and that's how my last time with the club ended.

I was then contacted by Keith Alexander who was now at Macclesfield Town with Gary Simpson. I was offered two mornings a week and two afternoons a week as part-time goalkeeping coach, for £640 a month. These were excellent terms and so I agreed immediately. I got on really well with Keith, having known him at Lincoln City. He was one of very few managers who understood the job of goalkeeper and frequently asked my advice, which I knew he listened to and took on board.

In February 2010 Keith had been suffering from hiccups that just wouldn't stop and I could see they were getting him down. I found him in his office once, lying down with all the lights out. I asked him if he was okay and insisted his son Matthew took him to hospital for a check. For one game I was assistant manager in his absence. We played Notts County at Meadow Lane on 2nd March and lost 1-0. Richard Butcher took Keith home from that game and Butch told me Keith had complained of feeling unwell all the way home. He died that night of a brain haemorrhage, aged fifty-three.

Our last game of the season was against Lincoln City on 8th May and we drew 0-0. It was on the way back home from Macclesfield that afternoon when I began feeling unwell. I had to stop the car several times, as I was sweating profusely and just didn't feel right. I knew something was seriously wrong. I was really concerned as I'd never felt like this before. I went to my doctor and was admitted to hospital immediately. I was diagnosed with atrial fibrillation, a heart condition that is often the cause of strokes. I was still only thirty-nine. It quickly worsened and I was soon unable to do anything, even the simplest of tasks. I was on a waiting list for a heart operation and when the opportunity came up after a cancellation I jumped at the chance. Luckily I made a full recovery.

The following year, on 9th January Butch didn't turn up for training and no-one knew why. Gary was now the manager and he asked Ben Futcher to go round to his house in Swinton to find him. He didn't answer the door so Ben rang the police. After confirming something was definitely wrong, they forced the front door. Butch was lying dead in bed; he was only twenty-nine. He had died in his sleep from heart problems.

Alan Marriott gave a speech to 3,000 people in a tribute to Butch at Sincil Bank. He said: 'Butch was a great friend to me. We used to car share and I remember on one occasion when it was his turn to drive, he stopped for fuel and only put five pounds in the car. I said to him "why only a fiver, Butch?" and he replied, "well, when I get home, my missus will go shopping in it and she'll fill it up!" Everyone laughed at this and I said to him afterwards 'Don't ever tell me you can't talk, Alan, because that was fantastic.'

It was this same awful year that my mum passed away. It wasn't a total surprise as she'd been battling cancer for many years, but it was still no less devastating. She'd been in a lot of pain and had bravely carried on until she was ninety-one.

Further huge changes to my private life followed. Julie and I could no longer continue our marriage after drifting apart and were divorced in 2012. I later married my current wife Fiona.

I worked again with John Ramshaw briefly at Arnold Town in Nottingham, but by this time I was forty-seven and my professional playing days were numbered. I couldn't dive for the ball any more or I'd probably break something when I hit the ground, unless I was doing one of my Norman Wisdom impressions of course. I knew I was more useful in the role of goalkeeping coach which by now I thoroughly enjoyed.

I'd lasted more than thirty years as a professional goalkeeper, since my first tentative appearance for Derby County in August 1977 for a few minutes against Millwall at The Den. I'd made 743 League appearances but now my life between the sticks was over. What an amazing career it has been.

I know I wasn't perfect but I did my best. I like to think that I gave good service to all the clubs I played for and it was a real honour and a privilege to play for my home town club.

Now I suppose I could always try earning a few bob from my Norman Wisdom impressions?

Anyway, cheers!